THE
MISSING
CENTER

THE MISSING CENTER

21 MODERN POLITICAL SPEECHES THAT UNITED AMERICA

Noah H. Harris

Skyhorse Publishing

Skyhorse Publishing books may be purchased in bulk at special discounts for sales promotion, corporate gifts, fund-raising, or educational purposes. Special editions can also be created to specifications. For details, contact the Special Sales Department, Skyhorse Publishing, 307 West 36th Street, 11th Floor, New York, NY 10018 or info@skyhorsepublishing.com.

Skyhorse® and Skyhorse Publishing® are registered trademarks of Skyhorse Publishing, Inc.®, a Delaware corporation.

Visit our website at www.skyhorsepublishing.com.

Please follow our publisher Tony Lyons on Instagram @tonylyonsisuncertain

10 9 8 7 6 5 4 3 2 1

Library of Congress Cataloging-in-Publication Data on file.

Cover design by L. Zolezzi S
Cover photograph by Siberian Art /Adobe Stock

Print ISBN: 978–1-5107–8280-8
Ebook ISBN: 978–1-5107–8285-3

Printed in the United States of America

CONTENTS

Dedicated to my father, Ben

AUTHOR'S NOTE

Select speeches were edited for formatting consistency
throughout the book.

INTRODUCTION

And that's how change happens in America. It doesn't happen on its own. It doesn't happen from on high. It happens from the bottom up. And breaking gridlock will come only when the American people demand it . . . only you can break this stalemate.

—Barack Obama, speaking on the Affordable Care Act, October 20, 2016

I n the first quarter of the twenty-first century, political, economic, and social issues have arisen that would have been unforeseeable to someone predicting the future at the start of the millennium. From 9/11 to the COVID-19 pandemic and disputed elections, the start of this century has seen significant challenges. During this period, the American people and our political leadership have become fractured. To many, it feels like the United States no longer has a shared set of values. All too often people retreat into factions of left and right, Democrat and Republican, liberal and conservative, and countless other self-described labels.

The challenge we face is how to get past today's culture of extreme partisanship to create an effective two-party system that does not grind the nation to gridlock with every policy debate. Legislators cannot agree on budgets, economic matters, immigration, education, social issues, or foreign affairs. In this climate, it is no surprise that the American public is losing faith in Washington's ability to govern. Fortunately, we do not have to look far to find examples from the past when this was not the case.

In a quest to find a path forward, *The Missing Center* showcases the transformative results that can happen when leaders govern from the center to unite, inspire, and solve complex problems. When elected officials run for office, they do so with a desire to help their constituents. Yet when many arrive in Washington, they become entangled in both inter- and intraparty political infighting. This is a relatively new occurrence and not how it has to be.

When a crisis occurs, the majority of politicians can generally put aside their differences and heed the call to lead. In times of urgency, inaction is not an option. After 9/11, politicians didn't speak to red or blue states but to the American public overall. They came together from both sides of the aisle to rise above partisanship. We have seen Republicans—traditionally the party of fiscal restraint—support high government spending to combat the economic impact of COVID-19 shutdowns, and we have seen Democrats—traditionally the less aggressive party on military intervention abroad—support U.S. involvement in conflicts in the Middle East following 9/11. This reminds us that government can solve complex problems when politicians arrive at consensus. My hope is that we can learn from these situations and make bipartisan policymaking the rule rather than the exception.

Speeches provide a useful framework to analyze the benefits of bipartisan governance. They help us see what good leadership looks like and how ideas that benefit the majority of Americans stand the test of time. Upon close examination, we find the common elements in effective political speeches are threefold. First, politicians address the public and explain the issue in terms everyone can understand. Second, they empathize with how the problem impacts people using concrete examples. Third, they propose an approach to solve the issue. Sometimes a solution to the root cause is impossible, but even then, effective politicians exhibit leadership by engaging in actions that mitigate damage and suffering.

We need to return to a bipartisan spirit in which the extreme flanks of both parties are tuned out. This is what will reunite our nation, showcase the impact of good governance, and help move us into the next stage of American civic life, beyond the vitriol and hatred for the other side we see too often today. Bipartisanship calls for civility in discussion with the tone set at the top levels of government for both officials and the public to emulate.

This book examines speeches delivered in response to the major issues of this century—cornerstone addresses in which the federal government responded to situations in humane terms and presented policy objectives within a centrist framework, with elements both parties can support. The legislation and policies proposed in these speeches came about thanks to bipartisan thinking. Many readers will likely agree with the policies advocated in these texts.

There have been many significant political moments in the twenty-first century. It was extremely difficult to choose only twenty-one speeches out of thousands. I have chosen to only use speeches by politicians while they were in office because the purpose of this book is to demonstrate the effectiveness of nonpartisan governing among elected officials who are in power, so it is relevant for the speeches to strictly be by governmental figures while they were in office.

In each chapter, I have provided the topic, speaker, and a transcript of the speech itself, prefaced by critical analysis to provide context and promote further evaluation. Collectively, the speeches represent important themes in modern America. You can reference the table of contents and read the speeches in the order of your choice based on your interest in the topics or in the order presented, which is chronological.

Some of the speeches are scheduled, such as State of the Union addresses or inaugural addresses, which are televised and delivered to large audiences. Others are ad hoc, often delivered to Congress or a politician's followers (plus the narrow audience of the CSPAN-obsessed) and focused on pressing events. Regardless of the size of the audience, these collected speeches are consistent in that a historian can see the rationale for government action and understand the mood and urgency of the occasion. If we think back to defining moments in the public sphere when a speech propelled an agenda forward, these typically represent the apex of a cause or concern. By studying them, we see that every day presents an opportunity for politicians to lead and drive meaningful change, even in today's hostile environment.

The speeches included in this anthology were chosen based on the following criteria:

1. The speech must address domestic or international politics, and, if international, must still pertain to the United States.
2. The speech must either have been inspired by an immediate need or overarching policy theme.
3. The speech must rise above partisanship, or at least support a position on which the majority of Americans could agree.
4. The speech must be from the twenty-first century.
5. The speech must have been delivered by a figure in public office.

The first speech included in this compilation is the only one that doesn't follow all of the guidelines, as it was not technically delivered in this century. Instead, it was delivered on New Year's Eve as we transitioned from the year 1999 to 2000, and ended one minute before this century began, at 11:59 p.m. This speech is included because it is solely about the twenty-first century—it offers a positive outlook on the coming hundred years and its optimism is interesting to consider in comparison to some of the challenging events that have occurred since the year 2000. The turn of the millennium was a time of great optimism and hope. The mood of the country a quarter of the way into the new century is anything but that. The goal of *The Missing Center* is to remind us that hope is not lost and that we only have to look to the recent past for lessons on how to achieve a better tomorrow.

The Results of Rising Above Partisanship

There have been moments in history when American society was fragmented and strong leadership pulled it back together. The Thirteen Colonies were not fully aligned prior to the American Revolution, but the Founding Fathers found enough areas for compromise to create a nation. Seventy-five years later, Abraham Lincoln managed to hold the core ideals of the nation together during the Civil War. Nearly three-quarters of a century after that, Franklin D. Roosevelt did the same by leading the United States out of the Great Depression, and later uniting Americans as the country entered World War II. Simply put, throughout U.S. history, strong leaders have been able to push partisan politics aside to effectively advance the interests of the nation.

Presidential candidates who appeal to centrist values have won elections from both sides of the aisle. Ronald Reagan, a staunch conservative, spoke of "American greatness." He won reelection with 59 percent of the popular vote and during his second term Reagan had a 68 percent approval rating. Bill Clinton campaigned on the theme of doing well for the greatest number of Americans and maintaining leadership in foreign affairs. At the height of his presidency, Clinton had a 73 percent approval rating.

Although Vietnam and Watergate led to strong policy differences between parties in the 1970s, Americans were not as politically polarized as we are today. The extreme era of modern partisanship began to intensify during the 1990s when Newt Gingrich and the Republican "Contract with America" changed the culture in Congress, employing new extreme partisan tactics against then-president Bill Clinton.

Partisanship has also increased in locales where one party has a decisive electoral majority. In these environments, elections become a competition within one party—not against the other—to determine who wins. This cycle creates voters who become more partisan over successive election cycles. As the Carnegie Endowment for International Peace explains, it is "a self-fulfilling prophecy: Voters exposed to more polarizing rhetoric from leaders who share their partisan identity are likely to alter their preferences based on their understanding of what their group believes and has normalized—particularly among primary voters whose identity is more tied to their party." It is commonly acknowledged that this requires candidates to generally take more extreme views to win their party primary, but it is not as well known that this makes voters more extreme as well. Hence, over time we see positions which seem archconservative in red states and overly progressive in blue ones.

This has resulted in greater disparities between the political middle, which most Americans subscribe to, and the far left and right. It has ramifications in Congress and in candidates for the presidency as the move away from the center gained steam. In the 2016 and 2020 presidential election cycles, Bernie Sanders, a progressive independent, became one of the leading candidates. Though he ultimately didn't win either primary, he influenced the Democratic Party's leftward shift as the party sought to attract his supporters. At the same time, Trump pulled voters from the far right and portions of the Republican party saw abortion and rollbacks of transgender rights as rallying cries to attract votes. Some of these ideas—which are not uniformly supported by centrist voters—became Republican party platform positions.

For decades, core Republican values centered on small government, championing the rights of the individual, low taxes, projecting American might overseas, and economic prosperity. While "culture war" issues existed, these were not the dominant theme of American politics. Today, hot issues have come to define political conversation. There will never be complete societal consensus on these issues, and the way culture war topics are framed in all-or-nothing rhetoric creates a predicament where those on the left and right feel they are losing ground by yielding to even the slightest compromise. Just discussing these topics creates a perceived threat to people's values and triggers antagonism toward the other side.

It would be ideal for a presidential candidate to unify the nation similarly to great leaders of the past by focusing on the vast number of matters on which we all agree. Such a conversation might be led by policies for a better educational system, economic prosperity, job growth, a strong military, codified immigration reform, a path to self-sufficiency for the disenfranchised, and a strong foreign policy to maintain America's status as a source of justice and a beacon of hope around the world. These issues are all within the purview of the federal government, and it seems that the majority of Americans would be receptive to such a return to the center. As the Carnegie Endowment for International Peace noted, "American voters are less ideologically polarized than they think they are, and that misperception is greatest for the most politically engaged people. Americans across parties share many policy preferences."

Foreign nations used to look to America as an enlightened country with a model of how to balance a strong central government with respect for local preferences. Peace, prosperity, and individual self-determination while respecting others are themes that date back to the founding of the nation and resonate equally well today. Bold leaders must break past the culture of extreme politicization by courting the missing center. George Washington, Thomas Jefferson, Franklin D. Roosevelt, and Harry S. Truman were able to unite. We can do this in modern times as well. In the pages that follow, we will see examples of politicians rising above the fray on important issues to achieve bipartisan consensus.

Public Opinion

Public opinion is extremely powerful. It can elect politicians, bring topics of conversation to the forefront, inspire movements, and change laws. Sometimes, matters of public opinion bring about immediate change; other times, the process is slower. Either way, the result is the same in that ideas that were outside the norm became the law of the land. The Civil Rights Movement of the 1960s brought racial justice to the forefront and resulted in a flurry of laws and policies to right past wrongs. The notion that all people deserve equal access to government services and equal opportunities went from an activist position to one accepted as a given.

Focusing on more recent events, there has been a growing movement in the twenty-first century supporting universal preschool, or pre-K, education. The benefits of pre-K are immense, yet such programs have historically been offered at mostly private and parochial schools which many families cannot afford. Although there are some public pre-K programs, these often have capacity constraints, in many places requiring a lottery for placement. As the benefits of early childhood education became better understood, this has added to America's tensions over economic inequality, particularly since children from families with greater economic means enroll in pre-K at higher rates than those living in poverty. In response to an unpleased citizenry, many localities have expanded their pre-K offerings and some in Congress have advocated for nationwide public preschool (see chapter 21). If the general trend continues, we can expect Congress to further address the issue of universal pre-K education in the years to come.

Another seismic shift in public opinion can be seen in views on health care. Medicare and Medicaid became law in 1965 and for many years were considered a sufficient federal response to the world of medicine. Nearly ten years into the twenty-first century, Barack Obama campaigned for president on the idea of reforming health care through what would become the Affordable Care Act, often referred to as Obamacare. Prior to his winning the presidency, healthcare reform was barely on the federal legislative agenda. It was thanks to a major shift in public opinion championed by then-candidate Obama that made the issue actionable. Once in office, President Obama reached across the aisle to get legislation passed, enacting numerous Republican themes in an olive branch that rose above partisanship. The result was that the uninsured rate in America dropped from 16 percent in 2010 to 9.1 percent in 2015, a difference of 20 million individuals.

Since the law's passage in 2010, public opinion on the matter has evolved and this has forced both parties' platforms to change as well. Today, while the left and right disagree on how to best implement government-sponsored insurance programs, the idea that this is within the purview of the federal government is no longer debated, at least by the majority of Americans. Chapter 12 explores how Obama championed the Affordable Care Act using his gift for public speaking to achieve historic outcomes.

Public opinion can turn issues that were once ignored into policy. It is an extremely powerful force which will hopefully be harnessed more frequently by those with centrist views in the future, rather than those on the extreme edges of the political spectrum.

Social Media

The advent of social media has increased the extreme polarization in politics. This is due to the prioritization of partisan viewpoints by algorithms that tend to divide users into self-contained echo chambers in which increasingly extreme voices are amplified. Internal documents from Facebook dated August 2019 that were leaked in a whistleblower action reported the site's awareness that:

> . . . our core product mechanics, such as virality, recommendations, and optimizing for engagement, are a significant part of why [hate] speech flourish[es] on the platform

> . . . the net result is that Facebook, taken as a whole, will
> be actively (if not necessarily consciously) promoting these
> types of activities. The mechanics of our platform are not
> neutral.

Similar criticism extends to other platforms—including TikTok and
YouTube—that rely on algorithms with a negative feedback loop.
Inflammatory content is shown with the goal of getting clicks,
thereby driving users, engagement, and revenue for the social media
platforms.

Additionally, because Facebook's algorithm deprioritizes the
user's exposure to conflicting views while progressively feeding the
user more of the types of content they engage with, the most partisan politicians—the progressive Squad for Democrats and Make
America Great Again (MAGA) for Republicans—tend to have posts
amplified well beyond the number of seats they have in Congress.
This extra-loud voice of the extremes does little to advance bipartisan legislation. Those who consume news through social media
find themselves in echo chambers where the same viewpoints are
repeated and they are not served information with opposing opinions. The platforms figure out which way you lean on a topic and
keep serving similar content. The ability to generate outrage maxi-
mizes clicks.

The short-form format of social media content is problematic on
many levels. Whereas Americans used to consume the news via mul-
tipage articles in newspapers and long segments on TV, social media
has reduced the world to a series of sound bites that typically lack context and almost never present an opposing view. Those who use social
media the most stay in echo chambers, form opinions often based
on false or incomplete information, and do not seek out the primary
sources because they feel the platform is delivering the "news." The
role of journalists to find trusted sources has been removed. Imagine
if people only saw a fifteen-second sound bite explaining America's

entry into World War I or World War II. Complex topics require longer explanations, which proper long-form speeches allow.

Although political speeches are still used often today, it is much more difficult for them to garner attention and an audience due to shortened attention spans and the fact that platforms might not serve the news of the day to all users (because serious things can be depressing and not generate as much revenue as a more entertaining post). When was the last time you went to CSPAN to watch a recording of a speech on an important topic? As a result, politicians have resorted to tweeting or posting their positions on issues, which forces an oversimplification of problems. There are many positive effects of social media, including the democratization of information, but being able to fully express complex ideas and to easily hear nuanced views from the other side are not among them.

Misinformation and Disinformation

There are two types of false information: misinformation and disinformation. According to the American Psychological Association, misinformation is simply "false or inaccurate information," whereas disinformation is "deliberately intended to mislead." In other words, people spreading misinformation aren't aware the information they are sharing is wrong, but people spreading disinformation are aware that the information is wrong and are purposefully spreading it to mislead. Using the example of the 2020 election, someone can genuinely believe and advocate for the fact that the election was stolen from Trump, making it misinformation, while someone who knows this is untrue but still argues this viewpoint would be spreading disinformation. Falsified photos and fake or misattributed quotes are common ways misinformation exhibits itself online, while forms of propaganda, such as incorrect news stories, posts, and deep fakes, are commonly disinformation.

Misinformation and disinformation have always been with us, but in the last few decades the opportunities to spread them have become much greater thanks to the internet and social media. In the past, journalists served as gatekeepers to information with an obligation to fact check. The internet removes the gatekeeper role and allows information (whether true or false) to spread at a much faster rate. Many social media users share disinformation and misinformation to promote their opinions. Such posts are then often shared by viewers who don't know the claims are false. In fact, one study found that fake news on Twitter spreads more rapidly than real news.

The solution to this would be to somehow police the internet. Many believe we should not do this, as it infringes on freedom of speech, and that it is possible social media companies will over-restrict one party's beliefs while letting the other side's flourish. Current law broadly protects social media companies from liability for misinformation and disinformation shared on their platforms. The United States is divided on how to handle this, and it will likely be a hot topic of conversation for a long time to come.

Agreeing on a shared set of facts to determine what is truth, what is misinformation, and what is disinformation is an integral first step to tackling an issue. Currently, politicians sometimes have viewpoints placed in such opposition that they can't even agree on the basic facts—they can't even agree what is true. This means that to Democrats, what Republicans are saying can be seen as false (be it misinformation or disinformation) when it is seen as factual to Republicans, or vice versa. Opinions have always been a part of the political process, but in the past the fundamental sets of facts to which politicians were responding were accepted by all. American democracy thrived for over two hundred years with opposing viewpoints but an agreed set of facts. Even controversial subjects relied on factual data. Until recently, the facts were not disputed. Debates were framed over whether and how the government should react to specific problems. Today, the left and right often cannot agree on a baseline set of facts.

We need to return to an environment where people can trust the news, separate fact from opinion, and have confidence in public institutions. Combating misinformation and disinformation should not be difficult. It simply relies on eliminating blatant falsehoods, honestly assessing areas where there is ambiguity, and returning to fact-based analysis, all while respecting and acknowledging opposing viewpoints. Parliamentary debate and today's two-party system came from this framework and the model has survived for centuries. *The Missing Center* reminds readers that the path to overcome today's challenges is well-known, embedded in our democracy, and within easy reach for those willing to embrace it.

Elected Office

Eloquent use of speech in politics can be extremely powerful and has a long-rooted tradition in America. *The Federalist Papers* were an early example of well-crafted essays that argued for the ratification of the Constitution. Since then, politicians have courted public opinion to advance policy positions, delivering addresses first in person, then by radio, TV, and now, live streaming. Regardless of the medium, speeches have framed pivotal moments in our nation's history. Abraham Lincoln's 1863 Gettysburg Address is one of the most-read speeches to this day.

With the advent of video-based mass media, oratory style changed. In one of the 1960 presidential debates, those listening by radio thought Richard Nixon had won, while those watching on TV thought the youthful, well-coiffed John F. Kennedy, Jr. had won. Ronald Reagan, Bill Clinton, and Barack Obama have been recognized as particularly effective communicators in their televised addresses. The House of Representatives and the Senate both revolve around elected officials' rhetorical abilities. For many years, CSPAN was the preferred outlet to deliver impassioned speeches. Ironically, many times such speeches were delivered in an empty room with the content later used as sound bites on the news or the campaign trail. Even so, public and political support of significant legislation comes about, in part, due to speeches. This means that the future of America can be shaped by the caliber of a speech. Officials know that to persuade Americans, a well-written address can rally support and move the undecided. This anthology includes many such persuasive speeches, hallmark addresses that frame significant moments of this century.

Elected office favors those who possess great oratory skills because it gives them the opportunity to use their abilities for a worthy cause. This has been the case for a long time, even in Ancient Athens, home to Pericles, one of the first recorded great public speakers in government. Pericles's speeches contributed significantly to the at-the-time novel concept of democracy, rallied the Greek army during the Greco-Persian Wars, and gave rise to the Parthenon. In fact, Pericles's influence in politics owing to his speaking abilities was so immense that he now has a time period, 461 to 429 BC, named after him: "The Age of Pericles." If one thing can be learned from Pericles, it is that great speech and oratory can successfully influence politics.

Speech and politics go well together. They can uplift, inspire, and bring cohesion to society. So far in the twenty-first century, skilled politicians have used powerful rhetoric to drive America forward, evidenced by the speeches in this book. Unfortunately, due to the rise of partisanship and social media, recent political discourse often lobs insults rather than focusing on progress and change. The goal of this book is to reset this. By returning to the missing center, we can find consensus-based policies and ideals that serve the test of time.

Hope for the Future

American politics is at a crossroads. Our system has resulted in a form of political gridlock wherein the extremes of both parties have undue influence over our nation's future. Many Americans view the presidential candidates of both major parties unfavorably. Due to partisanship, the democratic political experiment of the United

States of America is not living up to its potential. Now more than ever, we need to find a center that the nation can agree on.

The Missing Center shows that hope is not lost. Many unique problems have arisen in this new century, and the challenges we've done the best job solving required politicians to put aside their own political agendas in favor of mainstream solutions. We do not have to look to past centuries to see how to fix things. Despite the ever-darkening mood of political pundits, there are recent examples of good governance with great results. A lot of progress has been made on important topics. By exploring speeches which bring these themes to life, the tools and frameworks to improve the present situation become evident.

The Missing Center spotlights policy issues in which federal leaders tried to improve on the status quo and advance the interests of the nation, generally free from divisive partisan rhetoric. Some of the speeches were delivered at times of mourning and shock, others at times of peace and prosperity. No matter the occasion, topic, or side of the aisle the speaker came from, every speech included in this book advocates for change on an issue most people agree on. They are professional in tone and do not fit the confines of the internet's outrage apparatus. The best speeches—those that truly rise above partisanship—reach across the aisle, change minds, inspire, and unify the American public.

Today's bold leaders must move past the culture of extreme politicization by courting the missing center. This book showcases recent times when politicians used their rhetorical abilities to advance a common good, which can help restore faith in our institutions and democracy. Transformative results can happen when leaders set party aside to solve complex problems. *The Missing Center* reminds us that shared aspirations and goals have solved America's greatest challenges and are at the heart of our greatest accomplishments to come.

CHAPTER 1

Bill Clinton

America's Millennium Gala

1999

What will the story of the twenty-first century be? Let it be the triumph of freedom wisely used, to bring peace to a world in which we honor our differences, and even more, our common humanity.

President Bill Clinton addressed the nation on New Year's Eve to usher in the twenty-first century. It was a speech that marked not just the turn of the century, but the beginning of a new millennium.

Born in 1946, Clinton lived through the Civil Rights Movement, the end of the Cold War, and greater global cooperation. The world he grew up in had changed for the better during his lifetime.

Widely respected as a gifted orator, Clinton delivered an inclusive, forward-looking view on the promise of the country. He spoke about universal core values, reflected on progress from the past, and offered a vision of the society we might become.

Clinton's speech ended at 11:59 p.m. December 31, 1999, just one minute before the twenty-first century began. Although including this speech technically violates one of the tenets of this anthology—that speeches are from the twenty-first century—I believe it is important to include as it captures the mood of the time, particularly the sense that our best days were ahead. Clinton's New Year's Eve address was devoid of partisan reference, discussing American values and themes rarely heard in public discourse twenty-five years later.

The Clinton presidency took place at the start of the modern era of extreme partisanship. During his term, the nation saw a divided government with Republicans controlling both chambers of Congress, federal shutdowns, and an impeachment scandal that dominated the news cycle.

Despite this, leaders rose above the fray to appeal to the things that unite us. To readers of a certain age, this speech may trigger feelings of nostalgia. For younger readers, the language, tone, and mood may feel foreign. Regardless of your leaning, age, or experience, it is interesting to juxtapose this speech against the language politicians use today.

Americans were jubilant and excited for the future at the turn of the millennium. Clinton's address captures an incredible moment in time, one in which people generally thought America and the world were moving in a better direction. It reminds us to appreciate human achievement, to understand the progress from the past, and to believe in the promise of a better tomorrow.

———————

Ladies and gentlemen, tonight we celebrate. The change of centuries, the dawning of a new millennium are now just minutes away. We celebrate the past. We have honored America's remarkable achievements, struggles, and triumphs in the twentieth century. We celebrate the future, imagining an even more remarkable twenty-first century.

As we marvel at the changes of the last hundred years, we dream of what changes the next hundred, and the next thousand, will bring. And as powerful as our memories are, our dreams must be even stronger. For when our memories outweigh our dreams, we become old, and it is the eternal destiny of America to remain forever young, always reaching beyond, always becoming, as our founders pledged, a more perfect union. So we Americans must not fear change. Instead, let us welcome it, embrace it, and create it.

The great story of the twentieth century is the triumph of freedom and free people, a story told in the drama of new immigrants, the struggles for equal rights, the victories over totalitarianism, the stunning advances in economic well-being, in culture, in health, in space and telecommunications, and in building a world in which more than half the people live under governments of their own choosing, for the first time in all history. We must never forget the meaning of the twentieth century, or the gifts of those who worked and marched, who fought and died, for the triumph of freedom.

So as we ring in this new year, in a new century, in a new millennium, we must, now and always, echo Dr. King, in the words of the old American hymn, "Let freedom ring."

If the story of the twentieth century is the triumph of freedom, what will the story of the twenty-first century be? Let it be the triumph of freedom wisely used, to bring peace to a world in which we honor our differences, and even more, our common humanity. Such a triumph will require great efforts from us all. It will require us to stand against the forces of hatred and bigotry, terror and destruction. It will require us to continue to prosper, to alleviate poverty, to better balance the demands of work and family, and to serve each of us in our communities.

It will require us to take better care of our environment. It will require us to make further breakthroughs in science and technology, to cure dreaded diseases, heal broken bodies, lengthen life, and unlock secrets from global warming to the black holes in the universe. And, perhaps most important, it will require us to share—with our fellow Americans and, increasingly, with our fellow citizens of the world, the economic benefits of globalization; the political benefits of democracy and human rights; the educational and health benefits of all things modern, from the Internet to the genetic encyclopedia, to the mysteries beyond our solar system.

Now, we may not be able to eliminate all hateful intolerance, but we can develop a healthy intolerance of bigotry, oppression, and abject poverty. We may not be able to eliminate all the harsh consequences of globalization, but we can communicate more and travel more and trade more, in a way that lifts the lives of ordinary working families everywhere, and the quality of our global environment.

We may not be able to eliminate all the failures of government and international institutions, but we can certainly strengthen democracy so all children are prepared for the twenty-first-century world and protected from its harshest side effects. And we can do so much more to work together, to cooperate among ourselves, to seize the problems and the opportunities of this ever-small planet we all call home. In short, if we want the story of the twenty-first century to be the triumph of peace and harmony, we must embrace our common humanity and our shared destiny.

Now, we're just moments from that new millennium. Two centuries ago, as the framers were crafting our Constitution, Benjamin Franklin was often seen in Independence Hall looking at a painting of the sun low on the horizon. When, at long last, the Constitution finally was signed, Mr. Franklin, said: 'I have often wondered whether that sun was rising or setting. Today I have the happiness to know it is a rising sun.'

Well, two centuries later, we know the sun will always rise on America, as long as each new generation lights the fire of freedom. Our children are ready. So, again, the torch is passed—to a new century of young Americans!

CHAPTER 2

George W. Bush

State of the Union Address

2002

Steadfast in our purpose, we now press on. We have known freedom's price. We have shown freedom's power. And in this great conflict, my fellow Americans, we will see freedom's victor.

S tate of the Union addresses are annual speeches that allow the president to preview the agenda for the upcoming year and give the president the opportunity to speak to the entire nation at once. They are a useful tool to look back at specific moments in time and understand a president's thinking.

The 2002 State of the Union address was delivered four months after September 11, 2001, when terrorists hijacked four planes, crashing two into the World Trade Center and one into the Pentagon. The fourth aircraft crashed into a field in rural Pennsylvania after the passengers fought back against the hijacking. In total, 2,977 victims lost their lives to the 9/11 attacks, and many more were injured. This was the first large-scale attack by a foreign enemy on U.S. soil since Pearl Harbor, and it happened at what was perceived as a time of peace. The Cold War had ended just a decade earlier, and America was prosperous. This act of terrorism threw the United States into a state of disarray.

The speeches in this book revolve around the most consequential events of the twenty-first century, and 9/11 is one of the most traumatic moments not just in this century, but in U.S. history. It changed how America saw its role in the world, justified preventative action, and redefined its adversaries to include terrorist groups and non-state actors.

Coming on the heels of 9/11, the January 2002 State of the Union address stands out as a particularly defining moment. In this speech, President George W. Bush exhorts U.S. citizens to uphold American values, avenge the lives lost, and bring down terrorist cells. Bush speaks passionately to the hearts of Americans, rallying the nation and outlining plans for the Global War on Terror as a response to the tragedy of 9/11. He links bipartisan domestic legislative achievements with foreign policy goals such that the tone of the speech is one of unified resolve.

Today's reader may be critical of the length, tactics, and results of the War on Terror, but at the time, both Congress and public opinion were highly supportive of the need to take action. This speech is particularly noteworthy as it captures the bipartisan push for a response and the unified mood of the nation in the wake of 9/11, and inspired the nation to persevere.

———————

Mr. Speaker, Vice President Cheney, members of Congress, distinguished guests, fellow citizens: As we gather tonight, our nation is at war, our economy is in recession, and the civilized world faces unprecedented dangers. Yet the state of our Union has never been stronger.

We last met in an hour of shock and suffering. In four short months, our nation has comforted the victims, begun to rebuild New York and the Pentagon, rallied a great coalition, captured, arrested, and rid the world of thousands of terrorists, destroyed Afghanistan's terrorist training camps, saved a people from starvation, and freed a country from brutal oppression.

The American flag flies again over our embassy in Kabul. Terrorists who once occupied Afghanistan now occupy cells at Guantanamo Bay. And terrorist leaders who urged followers to sacrifice their lives are running for their own.

America and Afghanistan are now allies against terror. We'll be partners in rebuilding that country. And this evening we welcome the distinguished interim leader of a liberated Afghanistan: Chairman Hamid Karzai.

The last time we met in this chamber, the mothers and daughters of Afghanistan were captives in their own homes, forbidden from working or going to school. Today, women are free and are part of Afghanistan's new government. And we welcome the new Minister of Women's Affairs, Doctor Sima Samar.

Our progress is a tribute to the spirit of the Afghan people, to the resolve of our coalition, and to the might of the United States military. When I called our troops into action, I did so with complete confidence in their courage and skill. And tonight, thanks to them, we are winning the war on terror. The men and women of our armed forces have delivered a message now clear to every enemy of the United States: Even 7,000 miles away, across oceans and continents, on mountaintops and in caves—you will not escape the justice of this nation.

For many Americans, these four months have brought sorrow and pain that will never completely go away. Every day a retired firefighter returns to Ground Zero, to feel closer to his two sons who died there. At a memorial in New York, a little boy left his football with a note for his lost father: "Dear Daddy, please take this to heaven. I don't want to play football until I can play with you again someday."

Last month, at the grave of her husband, Michael, a CIA officer and Marine who died in Mazur-e-Sharif, Shannon Spann said these words of farewell: "Semper Fi, my love." Shannon is with us tonight.

Shannon, I assure you and all who have lost a loved one that our cause is just, and our country will never forget the debt we owe Michael and all who gave their lives for freedom.

Our cause is just, and it continues. Our discoveries in Afghanistan confirmed our worst fears and showed us the true scope of the task ahead. We have seen the depth of our enemies' hatred in videos, where they laugh about the loss of innocent life. And the depth of their hatred is equaled by the madness of the destruction they design. We have found diagrams of American nuclear power plants and public water facilities, detailed instructions for making chemical weapons, surveillance maps of American cities, and thorough descriptions of landmarks in America and throughout the world.

What we have found in Afghanistan confirms that, far from ending there, our war against terror is only beginning. Most of the nineteen men who hijacked planes on September the 11th were trained in Afghanistan's camps, and so were tens of thousands of others. Thousands of dangerous killers, schooled in the methods of murder, often supported by outlaw regimes, are now spread throughout the world like ticking time bombs, set to go off without warning.

Thanks to the work of our law enforcement officials and coalition partners, hundreds of terrorists have been arrested. Yet, tens of thousands of trained terrorists are still at large. These enemies view the entire world as a battle-field, and we must pursue them wherever they are. So long as training camps operate, so long as nations harbor terror-ists, freedom is at risk. And America and our allies must not, and will not, allow it.

Our nation will continue to be steadfast and patient and persistent in the pursuit of two great objectives. First, we will shut down terrorist camps, disrupt terrorist plans, and bring terrorists to justice. And second, we must pre-vent the terrorists and regimes who seek chemical, bio-logical, or nuclear weapons from threatening the United States and the world.

Our military has put the terror training camps of Afghanistan out of business, yet camps still exist in at least a dozen countries. A terrorist underworld—including groups like Hamas, Hezbollah, Islamic Jihad, [and] Jaish-e-Mohammed—operates in remote jungles and deserts and hides in the centers of large cities.

While the most visible military action is in Afghanistan, America is acting elsewhere. We now have troops in the Philippines, helping to train that country's armed forces to go after terrorist cells that have executed an American, and still hold hostages. Our soldiers, working with the Bosnian government, seized terrorists who were plotting to bomb our embassy. Our Navy is patrolling the coast of Africa to block the shipment of weapons and the establishment of terrorist camps in Somalia.

My hope is that all nations will heed our call and elim-inate the terrorist parasites who threaten their countries and our own. Many nations are acting forcefully. Pakistan is now cracking down on terror, and I admire the strong leadership of President Musharraf.

But some governments will be timid in the face of terror. And make no mistake about it: If they do not act, America will.

Our second goal is to prevent regimes that sponsor terror from threatening America or our friends and allies with weapons of mass destruction. Some of these regimes have been pretty quiet since September the 11th. But we know their true nature. North Korea is a regime arming with missiles and weapons of mass destruction, while starving its citizens. Iran aggressively pursues these weapons and exports terror, while an unelected few repress the Iranian people's hope for freedom. Iraq continues to flaunt its hostility toward America and to support terror. The Iraqi regime has plotted to develop anthrax, and nerve gas, and nuclear weapons for over a decade. This is a regime that has already used poison gas to murder thousands of its own citizens—leaving the bodies of mothers huddled over their dead children. This is a regime that agreed to international inspections—then kicked out the inspectors. This is a regime that has something to hide from the civilized world.

States like these, and their terrorist allies, constitute an axis of evil, arming to threaten the peace of the world. By seeking weapons of mass destruction, these regimes pose a grave and growing danger. They could provide these arms to terrorists, giving them the means to match their hatred. They could attack our allies or attempt to blackmail the United States. In any of these cases, the price of indifference would be catastrophic.

We will work closely with our coalition to deny terrorists and their state sponsors the materials, technology, and expertise to make and deliver weapons of mass destruction. We will develop and deploy effective missile defenses to protect America and our allies from sudden attack. And all nations should know: America will do what is necessary to ensure our nation's security.

We'll be deliberate, yet time is not on our side. I will not wait on events, while dangers gather. I will not stand by, as peril draws closer and closer. The United States of America will not permit the world's most dangerous regimes to threaten us with the world's most destructive weapons.

Our war on terror is well begun, but it is only begun. This campaign may not be finished on our watch—yet it must be, and it will be waged on our watch.

We can't stop short. If we stop now—leaving terror camps intact and terror states unchecked—our sense of security would be false and temporary. History has called America and our allies to action, and it is both our responsibility and our privilege to fight freedom's fight.

Our first priority must always be the security of our nation, and that will be reflected in the budget I send to Congress. My budget supports three great goals for America: we will win this war; we'll protect our homeland; and we will revive our economy.

September the 11th brought out the best in America, and the best in this Congress. And I join the American people in applauding your unity and resolve. Now Americans deserve to have this same spirit directed toward addressing problems here at home. I'm a proud member of my party—yet as we act to win the war, protect our people, and create jobs in America, we must act, first and foremost, not as Republicans, not as Democrats, but as Americans.

It costs a lot to fight this war. We have spent more than a billion dollars a month—over $30 million a day—and we must be prepared for future operations. Afghanistan proved that expensive precision weapons defeat the enemy and spare innocent lives, and we need more of them. We need to replace aging aircraft and make our military more agile, to put our troops anywhere in the world quickly and safely. Our men and women in uniform deserve the best weapons, the best equipment, the best training—and they also deserve another pay raise.

My budget includes the largest increase in defense spending in two decades—because while the price of freedom and security is high, it is never too high. Whatever it costs to defend our country, we will pay.

The next priority of my budget is to do everything possible to protect our citizens and strengthen our nation against the ongoing threat of another attack. Time and distance from the events of September the 11th will not make us safer unless we act on its lessons. America is no longer protected by vast oceans. We are protected from attack only by vigorous action abroad, and increased vigilance at home.

My budget nearly doubles funding for a sustained strategy of homeland security, focused on four key areas: bioterrorism, emergency response, airport and border security, and improved intelligence. We will develop vaccines to fight anthrax and other deadly diseases. We'll increase funding to help states and communities train and equip our heroic police and firefighters. We will improve intelligence collection and sharing, expand patrols at our borders, strengthen the security of air travel, and use technology to track the arrivals and departures of visitors to the United States.

Homeland security will make America not only stronger, but, in many ways, better. Knowledge gained from bioterrorism research will improve public health. Stronger police and fire departments will mean safer neighborhoods. Stricter border enforcement will help combat illegal drugs. And as government works to better secure our homeland, America will continue to depend on the eyes and ears of alert citizens.

A few days before Christmas, an airline flight attendant spotted a passenger lighting a match. The crew and passengers quickly subdued the man, who had been trained by al Qaeda and was armed with explosives. The people on that plane were alert and, as a result, likely saved nearly two hundred lives. And tonight, we welcome and thank flight attendants Hermis Moutardier and Christina Jones.

Once we have funded our national security and our homeland security, the final great priority of my budget is economic security for the American people. To achieve these great national objectives—to win the war, protect the homeland, and revitalize our economy—our budget will run a deficit that will be small and short-term, so long as Congress restrains spending and acts in a fiscally responsible manner. We have clear priorities, and we must act at home with the same purpose and resolve we have shown overseas: We'll prevail in the war, and we will defeat this recession.

Americans who have lost their jobs need our help, and I support extending unemployment benefits and direct assistance for health care coverage. Yet, American workers want more than unemployment checks—they want a steady paycheck. When America works, America prospers, so my economic security plan can be summed up in one word: jobs.

Good jobs begin with good schools, and here we've made a fine start. Republicans and Democrats worked together to achieve historic education reform so that no child is left behind. I was proud to work with members of both parties: Chairman John Boehner and Congressman George Miller. Senator Judd Gregg. And I was so proud of our work, I even had nice things to say about my friend, Ted Kennedy. I know the folks at the Crawford coffee shop couldn't believe I'd say such a thing—but our work on this bill shows what is possible if we set aside posturing and focus on results.

There is more to do. We need to prepare our children to read and succeed in school with improved Head Start and early childhood development programs. We must upgrade our teacher colleges and teacher training and launch a major recruiting drive with a great goal for America: a quality teacher in every classroom.

Good jobs also depend on reliable and affordable energy. This Congress must act to encourage conservation, promote technology, build infrastructure, and it must act to increase energy production at home so America is less dependent on foreign oil.

Good jobs depend on expanded trade. Selling into new markets creates new jobs, so I ask Congress to finally approve trade promotion authority. On these two key issues, trade and energy, the House of Representatives has acted to create jobs, and I urge the Senate to pass this legislation.

Good jobs depend on sound tax policy. Last year, some in this hall thought my tax relief plan was too small; some thought it was too big. But when the checks arrived in the mail, most Americans thought tax relief was just about right. Congress listened to the people and responded by reducing tax rates, doubling the child credit, and ending the death tax. For the sake of long-term growth and to help Americans plan for the future, let's make these tax cuts permanent.

The way out of this recession, the way to create jobs, is to grow the economy by encouraging investment in factories and equipment, and by speeding up tax relief so people have more money to spend. For the sake of American workers, let's pass a stimulus package.

Good jobs must be the aim of welfare reform. As we reauthorize these important reforms, we must always remember the goal is to reduce dependency on government and offer every American the dignity of a job.

Americans know economic security can vanish in an instant without health security. I ask Congress to join me this year to enact a patients' bill of rights; to give uninsured workers credits to help buy health coverage; to approve an historic increase in the spending for veterans' health; and to give seniors a sound and modern Medicare system that includes coverage for prescription drugs.

A good job should lead to security in retirement. I ask Congress to enact new safeguards for 401(k) and pension plans. Employees who have worked hard and saved all their lives should not have to risk losing everything if their company fails. Through stricter accounting standards and tougher disclosure requirements, corporate America must be made more accountable to employees and shareholders and held to the highest standards of conduct.

Retirement security also depends upon keeping the commitments of Social Security, and we will. We must make Social Security financially stable and allow personal retirement accounts for younger workers who choose them.

Members, you and I will work together in the months ahead on other issues: productive farm policy; a cleaner environment; broader homeownership, especially among minorities; and ways to encourage the good work of charities and faith-based groups. I ask you to join me on these important domestic issues in the same spirit of cooperation we've applied to our war against terrorism.

During these last few months, I've been humbled and privileged to see the true character of this country in a time of testing. Our enemies believed America was weak and materialistic, that we would splinter in fear and selfishness. They were as wrong as they are evil.

The American people have responded magnificently, with courage and compassion, strength and resolve. As I have met the heroes, hugged the families, and looked into the tired faces of rescuers, I have stood in awe of the American people.

And I hope you will join me—I hope you will join me in expressing thanks to one American for the strength and calm and comfort she brings to our nation in crisis, our First Lady, Laura Bush.

None of us would ever wish the evil that was done on September the 11th. Yet after America was attacked, it was as if our entire country looked into a mirror and saw our better selves. We were reminded that we are citizens, with obligations to each other, to our country, and to history. We began to think less of the goods we can accumulate, and more about the good we can do.

For too long our culture has said, "If it feels good, do it." Now America is embracing a new ethic and a new creed: "Let's roll." In the sacrifice of soldiers, the fierce brotherhood of firefighters, and the bravery and generosity of ordinary citizens, we have glimpsed what a new culture of responsibility could look like. We want to be a nation that serves goals larger than self. We've been offered a unique opportunity, and we must not let this moment pass.

My call tonight is for every American to commit at least two years—four thousand hours over the rest of your lifetime—to the service of your neighbors and your nation. Many are already serving, and I thank you. If you aren't sure how to help, I've got a good place to start. To sustain and extend the best that has emerged in America, I invite you to join the new USA Freedom Corps. The Freedom Corps will focus on three areas of need: responding in case of crisis at home; rebuilding our communities; and extending American compassion throughout the world.

One purpose of the USA Freedom Corps will be homeland security. America needs retired doctors and nurses who can be mobilized in major emergencies; volunteers to help police and fire departments; transportation and utility workers well-trained in spotting danger.

Our country also needs citizens working to rebuild our communities. We need mentors to love children, especially children whose parents are in prison. And we need more talented teachers in troubled schools. USA Freedom Corps will expand and improve the good efforts of AmeriCorps and Senior Corps to recruit more than 200,000 new volunteers.

And America needs citizens to extend the compassion of our country to every part of the world. So we will renew the promise of the Peace Corps, double its volunteers over the next five years—and ask it to join a new effort to encourage development and education and opportunity in the Islamic world.

This time of adversity offers a unique moment of opportunity—a moment we must seize to change our culture. Through the gathering momentum of millions of acts of service and decency and kindness, I know we can overcome evil with greater good. And we have a great opportunity during this time of war to lead the world toward the values that will bring lasting peace.

All fathers and mothers, in all societies, want their children to be educated, and live free from poverty and violence. No people on Earth yearn to be oppressed, or aspire to servitude, or eagerly await the midnight knock of the secret police.

If anyone doubts this, let them look to Afghanistan, where the Islamic "street" greeted the fall of tyranny with song and celebration. Let the skeptics look to Islam's own rich history, with its centuries of learning, and tolerance and progress. America will lead by defending liberty and justice because they are right and true and unchanging for all people everywhere.

No nation owns these aspirations, and no nation is exempt from them. We have no intention of imposing our culture. But America will always stand firm for the non-negotiable demands of human dignity: the rule of law; limits on the power of the state; respect for women; private property; free speech; equal justice; and religious tolerance.

America will take the side of brave men and women who advocate these values around the world, including the Islamic world, because we have a greater objective than eliminating threats and containing resentment. We seek a just and peaceful world beyond the war on terror.

In this moment of opportunity, a common danger is erasing old rivalries. America is working with Russia and China and India, in ways we have never before, to achieve peace and prosperity. In every region, free markets and free trade and free societies are proving their power to lift lives. Together with friends and allies from Europe to Asia, and Africa to Latin America, we will demonstrate that the forces of terror cannot stop the momentum of freedom.

The last time I spoke here, I expressed the hope that life would return to normal. In some ways, it has. In others, it never will.

Those of us who have lived through these challenging times have been changed by them. We've come to know truths that we will never question: Evil is real, and it must be opposed. Beyond all differences of race or creed, we are one country, mourning together and facing danger together. Deep in the American character, there is honor, and it is stronger than cynicism. And many have discovered again that even in tragedy—especially in tragedy—God is near.

In a single instant, we realized that this will be a decisive decade in the history of liberty, that we've been called to a unique role in human events. Rarely has the world faced a choice more clear or consequential.

Our enemies send other people's children on missions of suicide and murder. They embrace tyranny and death as a cause and a creed. We stand for a different choice, made long ago, on the day of our founding. We affirm it again today. We choose freedom and the dignity of every life.

Steadfast in our purpose, we now press on. We have known freedom's price. We have shown freedom's power. And in this great conflict, my fellow Americans, we will see freedom's victory.

Thank you all. May God bless.

CHAPTER 3

George W. Bush

Israel-Palestine Two-State Solution

2002

My vision is two states, living side by side in peace and security. There is simply no way to achieve that peace until all parties fight terror. Yet, at this critical moment, if all parties will break with the past and set out on a new path, we can overcome the darkness with the light of hope.

O n November 29, 1947, the United Nations passed Resolution 181, dividing the territories comprising Great Britain's Mandate for Palestine into independent Israeli and Palestinian states. The goal was for there to be two countries, peacefully coexisting side by side. Although Israel accepted Resolution 181, the Arab world rejected it, and, as a result, a Palestinian state was not created. Over the last three quarters of a century, there have been disputes over borders, the status of Jerusalem, and myriad other issues concerning the former Mandatory Palestine. A two-state solution has yet to arrive, with each side accusing the other of being the impediment to achieving lasting peace.

The goal of this chapter is not to be critical of either side. Rather, it is to stay true to the context of this book and recognize how well-framed public speeches can shape history by articulating shared values and goals to solve complex situations.

Numerous U.S. presidents and world leaders have tried to bring the sides together. The landmark 1993 Oslo Accords were perhaps one of the best attempts, in which Israeli and Palestinian leadership signed a Declaration of Principles intended to be a renewed road map to a two-state solution. Israel agreed to recognize the Palestine Liberation Organization as the official leader of the Palestinian people and to have Palestinian self-governance in the West Bank and Gaza.

In return, Palestinian leadership pledged to renounce terrorism, recognize Israel's right to exist, and to be on peaceful terms with its Jewish neighbor. Portions of the Israeli and Palestinian populations rejected the agreements, and in November 1995, Yitzhak Rabin, the Israeli Prime Minister who signed the documents, was assassinated by an Israeli who opposed the Accords.

In the year 2000, the second Palestinian Intifada (the al-Aqsa Intifada) began, and from 2000–2005 over one thousand Israelis and between three and five thousand Palestinians were killed. Even more were severely injured. As happens all too often, the promise of diplomacy failed to achieve its goals and new obstacles to peace emerged.

Nearly ten years later, President George W. Bush picked up where Clinton—who oversaw the signing of the Oslo Accords— left off, offering renewed hope for a solution to the conflict. Bush urged compromise between the two sides and recognized the issues both peoples face. His empathy for the Palestinians was at the time unprecedented; his offer of the endless support of the global community to the Palestinian people with the goal of ending the conflict between them and Israel was monumental. Despite the olive branch offered, a lasting settlement proved elusive once again.

In the twenty years since this speech was delivered, little headway has been made. The situation once again rose to world prominence on October 7, 2023, when Hamas launched a terrorist attack on Israel. It is within this context that Bush's 2002 speech has even greater meaning, as we see the progress that could have been made, and the crises averted, had Bush's vision for peace come to fruition.

For too long, the citizens of the Middle East have lived in the midst of death and fear. The hatred of a few holds the hopes of many hostage. The forces of extremism and terror are attempting to kill progress and peace by killing the innocent. And this casts a dark shadow over an entire region. For the sake of all humanity, things must change in the Middle East.

It is untenable for Israeli citizens to live in terror. It is untenable for Palestinians to live in squalor and occupation. And the current situation offers no prospect that life will improve. Israeli citizens will continue to be victimized by terrorists, and so Israel will continue to defend herself.

In this situation, the Palestinian people will grow more and more miserable. My vision is two states, living side by side in peace and security. There is simply no way to achieve that peace until all parties fight terror. Yet, at this critical moment, if all parties will break with the past and set out on a new path, we can overcome the darkness with the light of hope. Peace requires a new and different Palestinian leadership, so that a Palestinian state can be born.

I call on the Palestinian people to elect new leaders, leaders not compromised by terror. I call upon them to build a practicing democracy, based on tolerance and liberty. If the Palestinian people actively pursue these goals, America and the world will actively support their efforts. If the Palestinian people meet these goals, they will be able to reach agreement with Israel and Egypt and Jordan on security and other arrangements for independence.

And when the Palestinian people have new leaders, new institutions, and new security arrangements with their neighbors, the United States of America will support the creation of a Palestinian state whose borders and certain aspects of its sovereignty will be provisional until resolved as part of a final settlement in the Middle East.

In the work ahead, we all have responsibilities. The Palestinian people are gifted and capable, and I am confident they can achieve a new birth for their nation. A Palestinian state will never be created by terror—it will be built through reform. And reform must be more than cosmetic change, or veiled attempt to preserve the status quo. True reform will require entirely new political and economic institutions, based on democracy, market economics, and action against terrorism.

Today, the elected Palestinian legislature has no authority, and power is concentrated in the hands of an unaccountable few. A Palestinian state can only serve its citizens with a new constitution which separates the powers of government. The Palestinian parliament should have the full authority of a legislative body. Local officials and government ministers need authority of their own and the independence to govern effectively.

The United States, along with the European Union and Arab states, will work with Palestinian leaders to create a new constitutional framework, and a working democracy for the Palestinian people. And the United States, along with others in the international community, will help the Palestinians organize and monitor fair, multi-party local elections by the end of the year, with national elections to follow.

Today, the Palestinian people live in economic stagnation, made worse by official corruption. A Palestinian state will require a vibrant economy, where honest enterprise is encouraged by honest government. The United States, the international donor community, and the World Bank stand ready to work with Palestinians on a major project of economic reform and development. The United States, the E.U., the World Bank, the International Monetary Fund are willing to oversee reforms in Palestinian finances, encouraging transparency and independent auditing.

And the United States, along with our partners in the developed world, will increase our humanitarian assistance to relieve Palestinian suffering. Today, the Palestinian people lack effective courts of law and have no means to defend and vindicate their rights. A Palestinian state will require a system of reliable justice to punish those who prey on the innocent. The United States and members of the international community stand ready to work with Palestinian leaders to establish finance and monitor a truly independent judiciary.

Today, Palestinian authorities are encouraging, not opposing, terrorism. This is unacceptable. And the United States will not support the establishment of a Palestinian state until its leaders engage in a sustained fight against the terrorists and dismantle their infrastructure. This will require an externally supervised effort to rebuild and reform the Palestinian security services. The security system must have clear lines of authority and accountability and a unified chain of command.

America is pursuing this reform along with key regional states. The world is prepared to help, yet ultimately these steps toward statehood depend on the Palestinian people and their leaders. If they energetically take the path of reform, the rewards can come quickly. If Palestinians embrace democracy, confront corruption, and firmly reject terror, they can count on American support for the creation of a provisional state of Palestine.

With a dedicated effort, this state could rise rapidly, as it comes to terms with Israel, Egypt, and Jordan on practical issues, such as security. The final borders, the capital, and other aspects of this state's sovereignty will be negotiated between the parties, as part of a final settlement. Arab states have offered their help in this process, and their help is needed.

I've said in the past that nations are either with us or against us in the war on terror. To be counted on the side of peace, nations must act. Every leader actually committed to peace will end incitement to violence in official media, and publicly denounce homicide bombings. Every nation actually committed to peace will stop the flow of money, equipment, and recruits to terrorist groups seeking the destruction of Israel—including Hamas, Islamic Jihad, and Hezbollah. Every nation actually committed to peace must block the shipment of Iranian supplies to these groups, and oppose regimes that promote terror, like Iraq. And Syria must choose the right side in the war on terror by closing terrorist camps and expelling terrorist organizations.

Leaders who want to be included in the peace process must show by their deeds an undivided support for peace. And as we move toward a peaceful solution, Arab states will be expected to build closer ties of diplomacy and commerce with Israel, leading to full normalization of relations between Israel and the entire Arab world.

Israel also has a large stake in the success of a democratic Palestine. Permanent occupation threatens Israel's identity and democracy. A stable, peaceful Palestinian state is necessary to achieve the security that Israel longs for. So, I challenge Israel to take concrete steps to support the emergence of a viable, credible Palestinian state.

As we make progress towards security, Israeli forces need to withdraw fully to positions they held prior to September 28, 2000. And consistent with the recommendations of the Mitchell Committee, Israeli settlement activity in the occupied territories must stop.

The Palestinian economy must be allowed to develop. As violence subsides, freedom of movement should be restored, permitting innocent Palestinians to resume work and normal life. Palestinian legislators and officials, humanitarian and international workers, must be allowed to go about the business of building a better future. And Israel should release frozen Palestinian revenues into honest, accountable hands.

I've asked Secretary Powell to work intensively with Middle Eastern and international leaders to realize the vision of a Palestinian state, focusing them on a comprehensive plan to support Palestinian reform and institution-building.

Ultimately, Israelis and Palestinians must address the core issues that divide them if there is to be a real peace, resolving all claims and ending the conflict between them. This means that the Israeli occupation that began in 1967 will be ended through a settlement negotiated between the parties, based on U.N. Resolutions 242 and 338, with Israeli withdrawal to secure and recognized borders.

We must also resolve questions concerning Jerusalem, the plight and future of Palestinian refugees, and a final peace between Israel and Lebanon, and Israel and a Syria that supports peace and fights terror.

All who are familiar with the history of the Middle East realize that there may be setbacks in this process. Trained and determined killers, as we have seen, want to stop it. Yet the Egyptian and Jordanian peace treaties with Israel remind us that with determined and responsible leadership progress can come quickly.

As new Palestinian institutions and new leaders emerge, demonstrating real performance on security and reform, I expect Israel to respond and work toward a final status agreement. With intensive effort by all, this agreement could be reached within three years from now. And I and my country will actively lead toward that goal.

I can understand the deep anger and anguish of the Israeli people. You've lived too long with fear and funerals, having to avoid markets and public transportation, and forced to put armed guards in kindergarten classrooms. The Palestinian Authority has rejected your offer at hand and trafficked with terrorists. You have a right to a normal life; you have a right to security; and I deeply believe that you need a reformed, responsible Palestinian partner to achieve that security.

I can understand the deep anger and despair of the Palestinian people. For decades you've been treated as pawns in the Middle East conflict. Your interests have been held hostage to a comprehensive peace agreement that never seems to come, as your lives get worse year by year. You deserve democracy and the rule of law. You deserve an open society and a thriving economy. You deserve a life of hope for your children. An end to occupation and a peaceful democratic Palestinian state may seem distant, but America and our partners throughout the world stand ready to help, help you make them possible as soon as possible.

If liberty can blossom in the rocky soil of the West Bank and Gaza, it will inspire millions of men and women around the globe who are equally weary of poverty and oppression, equally entitled to the benefits of democratic government.

I have a hope for the people of Muslim countries. Your commitments to morality, and learning, and tolerance led to great historical achievements. And those values are alive in the Islamic world today. You have a rich culture, and you share the aspirations of men and women in every culture. Prosperity and freedom and dignity are not just American hopes, or Western hopes. They are universal, human hopes. And even in the violence and turmoil of the Middle East, America believes those hopes have the power to transform lives and nations.

This moment is both an opportunity and a test for all parties in the Middle East: an opportunity to lay the foundations for future peace; a test to show who is serious about peace and who is not. The choice here is stark and simple. The Bible says, "I have set before you life and death; therefore, choose life." The time has arrived for everyone in this conflict to choose peace, and hope, and life.

Thank you very much.

CHAPTER 4

George W. Bush

The No Child Left Behind Act

2003

The era of low expectations and low standards is ending; a time of great hopes and proven results is arriving. And together, we are keeping a pledge: every child in America will learn, and no child will be left behind.

W hen it was passed in 2002, The No Child Left Behind Act (NCLB) was credited as the most ambitious federal education legislation of the past forty years. It received bipartisan support at a time when Americans were upset that the public school system was not keeping up with its global peers. It was widely believed that if left unaddressed, the ramifications of failing schools would reduce American competitiveness and result in the failure of public education to serve the needs of students and families.

NCLB is particularly notable because it was championed by a Republican president. Traditionally, Republicans have favored smaller government and have not placed education at the top of their priority list. President George W. Bush campaigned on "compassionate conservatism" and felt that uplifting the lives of students, particularly those from minority and disadvantaged backgrounds, was important. NCLB was opposed by teacher unions but held wide support among the general public at the time of its passing. The legislation stands as an example of the federal government pushing the nation to achieve higher educational goals. It offered families hope that the government had remedies to improve public schools and promised measurable results by increasing accountability from states and individual schools. NCLB triggered a short-term increase in math proficiency rates, however, some felt it placed too much emphasis on teaching to standardized tests.

Bush's speech one year after the passage of NCLB highlights the difficult path getting the legislation through Congress. Bush thanks Democratic congressional leaders, specifically citing that this legislation is bipartisan and puts the interests of American students first. This acknowledgment shows the promise of the executive and legislative branches working together across the aisle to solve problems which, if left unaddressed, would fester.

Under Bush's leadership, NCLB merged core elements of the ideologies of the right and left: support for education has historically been a key issue for Democrats; the ability to interpret federal legislation on a local level key for Republicans. While no large-scale initiative is perfect, NCLB renewed the government's commitment to support quality education and shows a time when both sides came together to advance shared interests.

Welcome to the White House and the beautiful Rose Garden. I want to thank you for coming today to help us mark progress, significant progress, toward making sure our public schools meet our objective, which is [that] every single child in America gets a high-quality education.

Last year, I had the honor of signing into law some historic reforms. The No Child Left Behind Act sets a clear objective for American education. Every child in every school must be performing at grade level in the basic subjects that are key to all learning, reading and math. The ambitious goal is the most fundamental duty of every single school, and it must, and it will be fulfilled.

In order to ensure this goal is met, the No Child Left Behind Act requires every state in our country to submit an accountability plan that leads to measurable gains in student performance. As of today, all of the states, plus Puerto Rico and the District of Columbia, have now submitted those plans. And that's why we're meeting.

The era of low expectations and low standards is ending; a time of great hopes and proven results is arriving. And together, we are keeping a pledge: Every child in America will learn, and no child will be left behind.

For too many years, education reform seemed like a losing battle. Fads came and fads went while students were passed from grade to grade, no matter what they did or did not learn. And as a result, national tests showed that fewer than one in three fourth graders were reading well and that only four in ten high school seniors were skilled at reading. Because we were just simply shuffling kids through the system, we began to pay a serious price.

But fortunately, we recognized the problem, and we acted. I say we—it's not only Republicans but Democrats. All of us came together to focus on a significant problem for our country. We are now directly challenging the soft bigotry of low expectations. Under the No Child Left Behind Act, every student in this country will be held to high standards, and every school will be held accountable for results. Teachers will get the training they need to help their students achieve. Parents will get the information and choices they need to make sure their children are learning. And together we will bring the promise of quality education to every child in America.

Part of the answer is funding, and we are meeting our obligations here in Washington, DC. The federal government is investing more money in elementary and secondary education than at any other time in American history. The budget for next year boosts education funding to $53.1 billion and an increase of nearly $11 billion since I took office. And it wasn't all that long ago that I took office. Funding for Title I, a program that helps our most disadvantaged students, has increased 33 percent to $11.6 billion. And since I took office, we've tripled the amount we're spending on effective reading programs to more than $1 billion.

At the federal level, we are putting money into the system. It is also important for our fellow citizens to understand that there is money available for states to put in accountability systems, for states to train teachers in the methods that work, and for states to provide extra help to students who need it.

But it's also important to recognize that pouring money into systems that do not teach and refuse to change will not help our children. We help children by measuring the educational progress of every single child and by insisting on change when progress is not made. We're spending more money on schools, but the change is we're now asking for results. And those results must be proven, and those results must be measured every single year.

Success comes when we've got strong leadership in our schools—leaders who seek the truth, leaders who are willing to confront reality, and leadership who believes in the worth of every single child. And we have such a leader with us today. Linda Reksten is with us today. Linda is the principal of Disney Elementary School in Burbank, California. It's a Title I school where half the students are not fluent in English and nearly two-thirds come from low-income families.

Four years ago, her students scored at the 40th and 44th percentiles for reading comprehension and math on the state tests. And her school wound up on a list of under-performing schools. At first, Linda said she and her teachers felt powerless, felt overwhelmed. But they overcame their discouragement and got to work.

And here's what Disney School did. They began a rigorous testing program to measure the progress of every child several times a year. Teachers who had initially been skeptical of the tests—and I'm sure the state leaders here have heard of that skepticism before—learned how to use test results to tailor their lesson plans and to make sure every child excelled. Morale went up. Discipline problems went down. And last year, Disney students scored at the 58th percentile in reading comprehension and the 71st percentile in math. And that is tremendous progress.

And let me tell you what Linda said. She said, "It is this constant assessment that tells us what to do next. Once we have the test data and we know where the gaps are, we go after the gaps. We know where every child is." Linda is right. She has shown what works in education. She is the model of education reform. I'm proud you're here. Thank you for your leadership, and thank you for your heart.

The core of the No Child Left Behind legislation is that every child must be tested on the basics, starting early, because testing shows what children are learning and where they need help. We also need to train the teachers in scientifically proven methods of teaching the basics so that their students can make progress. And if the basics are not being taught and our children are not meeting standards, schools must be held to account. There must be a consequence. The status quo if a school is mediocre is not acceptable.

We're making good progress in terms of the implementation of our accountability systems. In the past five months, we have approved the accountability plans of thirty-three states, plus the District of Columbia and Puerto Rico. And today we mark an historic milestone of accountability. This morning, Secretary Paige has approved the plans of seventeen more states, bringing us to a total of 100 percent of the accountability plans in place.

I want to thank the Secretary, his staff, and education chiefs for helping this nation make great progress when it comes to education reform. Keep in mind that in January of 2001, only eleven states were in compliance with a 1994 education law. Every state, plus Puerto Rico and the District, are now complying with the No Child Left Behind Act after one year.

Educators are embracing a new level of accountability, which is creating a new culture for our nation's schools, a culture of achievement, a culture of results over process. In this new culture, accountability plans are driving reform. They contain timelines and projections to show how the states will bring all students up to grade level in reading and math by the year 2014. All students will be tested: tests designed by the states, not the federal government. Schools are required to disaggregate the testing data, separating the results by race and background to make sure all groups of children are learning. All schools must release report cards with these results to the parents and to the public, so we know which schools are succeeding and which schools are not.

Though the plans have these common elements, each plan is unique, because each state and its communities are unique. Local people are getting the tools they need to find out if children are learning and if their schools are working. Local people are charting the path to excellence, and that is important because local people know what is best for their own children and their own schools.

The development of these plans involved a lot of hard work. Governors stepped up to the line, along with their education chiefs. I also want to thank the principals and teachers and parents on the frontlines who are working so hard to improve our public schools. Instead of throwing up your hands in despair, you decided to challenge the status quo and to help each child. On behalf of the nation, I want to thank all who are involved in America's public schools, all who demand excellence, for your service to our country.

And now we look forward to the next phase of school reform. The law requires every state to release a list of its schools in need of improvement before the start of the school year. The schools on those lists are immediately eligible for state assistance that can help them improve. The school remains on the list for two years. Parents will have the option of moving their children to other public schools in the same district. If a school stays on the list for three years, a parent will be given a choice of tutoring programs with proven track records, programs in which they can enroll their children at no cost.

The No Child Left Behind Act gives parents and students alternatives when schools do not measure up. Some of those schools will undoubtedly have to make difficult choices. That's okay. Remember what's at stake. When a student passes from grade to grade without knowing how to read and write, add and subtract, the damage can last a lifetime. We must not tolerate a system that just gives up on a child early. We must not tolerate tired excuses. We must challenge persistent failure. And that is precisely what this nation is going to do. We are insisting on high standards and high achievement for every school in every corner of America because we have a fundamental belief that every child can learn in this country.

It's an exciting time for American education—it really is. We're facing challenges, but we have the blueprint for success. The No Child Left Behind Act charts the way for a better tomorrow. We've also got a greater advantage than the law. We have got the will and the character of the American people. Parents and teachers and principals and education chiefs are making good on our promise to leave no child left behind. We will continue to stand with them as they help the next generation realize the greatness of our country.

And we do live in a great country, a country of great values, a country of hope, a country that believes in the best for every single citizen who lives in our land.

May God bless your work, and may God continue to bless the United States of America.

CHAPTER 5

_____

James Greenwood

Medicare Prescription Drug, Improvement, and Modernization Act

2003

We need to modernize Medicare. As long as Medicare does not cover outpatient drug benefits, seniors will not be as healthy as they could be, and they will pay more out–of–pocket costs for preventive medications. . . . We owe it to our seniors to pass and have the president sign into law a prescription drug benefit this year.

_____

Medicare and Social Security are two large-scale government programs providing benefits to senior citizens. The fact that all citizens over a certain age (currently sixty-seven for Social Security and sixty-five for Medicare) are covered by these programs has made them cornerstones of the federal government as there are few other programs which touch the lives of so many people. Many Americans have come to view these entitlement programs as sacrosanct in our nation's laws. People pay into these programs via taxes during their working years and receive benefits during retirement. Significant changes to the programs are few and far between due to cost, political calculations of not wanting to alienate a large voting bloc, and the fact that many young and middle-aged people look forward to receiving the benefits themselves.

Medicare was founded in 1965 to provide health care to our nation's seniors. It became generally popular and is now the center-piece of the federal social safety net. In the nearly forty years since Medicare began, there were major advancements in medicine with entire new classes of drugs being able to extend life, relieve maladies, and treat sickness. American life expectancy had risen dramatically between 1965 to 2003, thanks in part to advances in screening, treatment, and prevention. However, many senior citizens still could not afford prescription drugs.

It is often Democrats who are thought of as promoting large-scale social initiatives, but the hallmark Medicare Prescription Drug, Improvement, and Modernization Act of 2003, also known as the Medicare Modernization Act, was championed by the Bush White House and Republican lawmakers on Capitol Hill, including House Representative Jim Greenwood, a six-term Republican representing Northeastern Pennsylvania. The Medicare Modernization Act finally brought Medicare up to the standards of modern medicine by offering an affordable prescription drug benefit plan for older Americans.

As with any large-scale government program, there were concerns about how the law was written and unintended consequences. Republican House leadership was criticized for working too closely with the AARP and the medical establishment, but their view was that input from stakeholders in the medical system was necessary. Prior efforts conceived in a vacuum on Capitol Hill had failed to take hold. The result was a significant piece of legislation that created better benefits and quality of life for our nation's senior citizens.

The speech that follows is from Greenwood, who articulates the benefits of the Medicare Modernization Act. His ability to make a complex issue relatable, including discussing criticisms of the law and why these were unfounded, is an example of a congressman using the House floor to deliver a meaningful speech in support of one of the most impactful pieces of legislation of modern times. Considering the hundreds of millions of people who have benefited from this law, plus the hundreds of millions more who will in the future as they age into coverage eligibility, this is a significant speech for a significant act which finally brought Medicare in line with twenty-first-century medical care.

Mr. Speaker, I support this new, innovative Medicare prescription drug benefit and commend Energy and Commerce Committee Chairman Tauzin and Health Subcommittee Chairman Bilirakis for developing a proposal that is fiscally responsible, modernizes the Medicare program, and delivers a sound prescription drug benefit.

A prescription drug benefit in Medicare is the most important social policy that Congress can deliver this Congress. Period.

My home state of Pennsylvania has the second-highest number of seniors in the country, and these seniors are living longer, healthier lives, thanks in part to modern medications. Death rates from heart disease, cancer, and stroke are going down, and hundreds of new medications are now being developed to combat diseases of aging, including Alzheimer's, Parkinson's, and arthritis.

Unfortunately, along with these new drug therapies comes a higher price to those that need them. Seniors without adequate access to these drugs will not be able to

benefit from the stunning advances in health care resulting from the newest pharmaceutical products. Society will
spend more money on their health care, because many new
drugs actually serve as preventive measures and often prevent costly hospitalizations. Medicare in its current form
does not cover most prescription drugs.

When it was created in 1965, it was a good program for
its time. President Johnson, on signing Medicare into law
on July 30, 1965, said, "No longer will older Americans be
denied the healing miracle of modern medicine. No longer will illness crush and destroy the savings they have so
carefully put away over a lifetime so that they might enjoy
dignity in their later years."

But with advancements in drug treatment, modern
medicine has grown increasingly expensive, as Medicare
does not pay for these wonderful outpatient drugs. We
need to modernize Medicare. As long as Medicare does
not cover outpatient drug benefits, seniors will not be as
healthy as they could be, and they will pay more out-of-
pocket costs for preventive medications.

Nearly two-thirds of seniors have some insurance coverage that helps pay for prescription drugs through private
employer plans or supplemental (Medigap) coverage; however, the remaining third has absolutely no coverage for
prescription drugs.

This is not good enough. Seniors, living on limited
income, should not be the last payers of retail prices for
drugs in our great country. But we should not impose
price controls so that seniors can afford their prescrip-
tions. Instead, we need to use the tools that the private
sector does, using leverage and bargaining for discounts.
Medicare needs to take advantage of reduced prices that
we can achieve using the tools that are used by private

entities, operating in the employer-provided health care market.

We need to be careful about how we reform Medicare. Those two-thirds of seniors who have drug coverage are pleased with what coverage they have and don't want a big government solution that could increase their costs. Congress passed the Medicare Catastrophic Coverage Act in 1988 with the intention of easing the cost of catastrophic events for Medicare recipients. However, instead of helping, it made things much worse for seniors who already had catastrophic coverage. They ended up paying more out of pocket for fewer health benefits. It was so devastating that Congress was forced to repeal the legislation the very next year.

Mr. Speaker, this bill finds the right mix. It establishes a generous prescription drug benefit, using the private-sector tools that provide significant savings for seniors when they purchase prescription drugs. And it reforms and strengthens the Medicare program in the right way. This bill also provides significant relief to seniors in Pennsylvania by strengthening the Medicare+Choice program. Over the past few years, seniors who have enrolled in Medicare+Choice have seen programs increase their premiums, decrease their benefits, or leave the program altogether. For example, in the largest plan in my district, seniors have seen their premiums rise from $0 to $94 per month.

This bill stabilizes the Medicare+Choice program. And it fundamentally reforms the program by creating the "MedicareAdvantage" program. This program provides for significantly more stability by allowing for competitive bidding by the plans. The MedicareAdvantage program will help these plans so that they remain a viable option for millions of seniors, and continue to provide a variety of health services, such as vision, hearing, and preventative care that are not offered through the traditional Fee for Service program.

Mr. Speaker, let me talk for a minute about the reforms in the bill. It provides for the creation of a new enhanced fee-for-service program that gives beneficiaries new options and choices for services. Finally, the Medicare program will incorporate the most popular option in private health insurance (and the health insurance offered in the Federal Employees Health Benefits program), preferred provider organizations (PPO). These new PPOs will create significant new options for services for seniors.

Furthermore, this bill will not only include improving access to prescription drugs, but will modernize the Medicare program by increasing the availability of wellness programs and streamlining the often-cumbersome paperwork that seniors face in getting Medicare benefits.

Finally, I am pleased that H.R. 1 has included provisions to reform the payments for the drugs that Medicare does cover in Part B. These reforms represent the culmination of a multi-year investigation by the Energy and Commerce Committee.

Presently, providers are reimbursed for the cost of these drugs at 95 percent of the average wholesale price (AWP). Congress and Medicare officials have wrestled for years with the difficult issue of how to set a fair and appropriate Medicare reimbursement rate for prescription drugs covered by Medicare Part B. The reimbursement benchmark we have used since the early 1990s has been the AWP, which is reported by drug companies and price reporting services. Prior to that, providers were reimbursed on a cost basis, which is cumbersome and inflationary.

Over the past decade, what we have learned is that the AWP is a fictitious number that must be changed. Rather than an accurate barometer of the price at which physicians purchase the drugs used in their practice, the AWP benchmark is more like a car's sticker price, which is usually much higher than the actual acquisition cost.

Under competitive pressure, manufacturers and wholesalers will routinely discount drug prices to physicians, lower their cost, while maintaining a higher AWP. In a competitive spiral, these discounts grow, increasing the net profits on the drugs, while the Medicare program continues to pay the higher AWP.

Unfortunately, due to the 20 percent co-pay that all beneficiaries pay for Part B services, Medicare beneficiaries presently pay $200 million more than they should in inflated co-pays. What's more, the Medicare program itself pays over $1 billion more than we should. The new system, based on competitive bidding and choice, pays appropriately for drugs and reimburses physicians appropriately for services. Under this new model, we provide physicians a choice—either continue to do business as they have or enter a new program that provides drugs to physicians for administration on a replacement basis. These reforms are fair, sound, and must be enacted.

Earlier this year, Congress set aside $400 billion for the development of a prescription drug benefit in Medicare. This is a significant and meaningful commitment by Congress for our nation's seniors. Some may quibble about the size of the benefit. However, I am convinced that we can pass legislation so that every senior has access to the latest prescription drug products and has catastrophic coverage for very serious, very costly medical conditions. We owe it to our seniors to pass and have the president sign into law a prescription drug benefit this year.

CHAPTER 6

Barack Obama

Inaugural Address

2009

The question we ask today is not whether our government is too big or too small, but whether it works. . . . Where the answer is yes, we intend to move forward. Where the answer is no, programs will end. And those of us who manage the public's dollars will be held to account, to spend wisely, reform bad habits, and do our business in the light of day, because only then can we restore the vital trust between a people and their government.

Inaugural addresses are almost always used to inspire Americans to believe that the best days are ahead. The newly elected president outlines a vision for the future and establishes a tone of unity with promises to represent the best interests of those who voted for them as well as their opponent. In the 2008 election, Barack Obama campaigned on hope, progress, and change, with the slogans "Change we can believe in" and "Yes, we can!" His opponent,

Senator John McCain, was a dedicated war veteran with a long career in public service. Like elections today, the tone of the campaigns turned divisive with what was then record-setting advertising spending combined with a near-record level of negative messaging. Obama wound up winning the election thanks in large part to the youth vote and his campaign's idealistic tone that suggested America's best days were yet to come.

President Obama came to the White House at a difficult time for America. His administration was tasked with solving the global financial crisis, wars in the Middle East, the issue of expensive health care, the general feeling that America was losing its place in the world, and a gloomy national mood.

Obama's inaugural address follows the model of some of the best bipartisan speeches by public officials. He acknowledges the pains felt by voters and outlines the shortcomings of the federal government, then changes the tone to offer solutions and reassure the nation that America will remain strong. Obama reflects on the difficult past our country has endured and how through tough times, perseverance, vision, and a commitment to shared values modeled by the founders of the Republic, America has overcome past challenges. Obama reached across the aisle to acknowledge the Republican critique that government had become too big and offered voters accountability and transparency.

Obama is widely recognized as a gifted orator. His choice of words and nuanced delivery style set him apart. Regardless of whether people agree with his policies, many still acknowledge his ability to connect with the American people and use of language are among his gifts. This speech is a perfect example of what an inaugural address should be. It overcomes partisanship and promotes unity. Obama projects confidence in his and Congress's leadership abilities with the uplifting message the nation needed at the time—namely, that our best days are still ahead.

My fellow citizens: I stand here today humbled by the task before us, grateful for the trust you've bestowed, mindful of the sacrifices borne by our ancestors.

I thank President Bush for his service to our nation as well as the generosity and cooperation he has shown throughout this transition.

Forty-four Americans have now taken the presidential oath. The words have been spoken during rising tides of prosperity and the still waters of peace. Yet, every so often, the oath is taken amidst gathering clouds and raging storms. At these moments, America has carried on not simply because of the skill or vision of those in high office, but because we, the people, have remained faithful to the ideals of our forebears and true to our founding documents.

So it has been; so it must be with this generation of Americans.

That we are in the midst of crisis is now well understood. Our nation is at war against a far-reaching network of violence and hatred. Our economy is badly weakened, a consequence of greed and irresponsibility on the part of some, but also our collective failure to make hard choices and prepare the nation for a new age. Homes have been lost, jobs shed, businesses shuttered. Our health care is too costly, our schools fail too many—and each day brings further evidence that the ways we use energy strengthen our adversaries and threaten our planet.

These are the indicators of crisis, subject to data and statistics. Less measurable, but no less profound, is a sapping of confidence across our land; a nagging fear that America's decline is inevitable, that the next generation must lower its sights.

Today, I say to you that the challenges we face are real. They are serious and they are many. They will not be met easily or in a short span of time. But know this, America: they will be met.

On this day, we gather because we have chosen hope over fear, unity of purpose over conflict and discord. On this day, we come to proclaim an end to the petty grievances and false promises, the recriminations and worn-out dogmas that for far too long have strangled our politics. We remain a young nation. But in the words of Scripture, the time has come to set aside childish things. The time has come to reaffirm our enduring spirit; to choose our better history; to carry forward that precious gift, that noble idea passed on from generation to generation: the God-given promise that all are equal, all are free, and all deserve a chance to pursue their full measure of happiness.

In reaffirming the greatness of our nation, we understand that greatness is never a given. It must be earned. Our journey has never been one of shortcuts or settling for less. It has not been the path for the fainthearted, for those that prefer leisure over work, or seek only the pleasures of riches and fame. Rather, it has been the risk-takers, the doers, the makers of things—some celebrated, but more often men and women obscure in their labor—who have carried us up the long, rugged path towards prosperity and freedom.

For us, they packed up their few worldly possessions and traveled across oceans in search of a new life. For us, they toiled in sweatshops, and settled the West, endured the lash of the whip, and plowed the hard earth. For us, they fought and died in places like Concord and Gettysburg, Normandy and Khe Sanh.

Time and again these men and women struggled and sacrificed and worked till their hands were raw so that we might live a better life. They saw America as bigger than the sum of our individual ambitions, greater than all the differences of birth or wealth or faction.

This is the journey we continue today. We remain the most prosperous, powerful nation on Earth. Our workers are no less productive than when this crisis began. Our minds are no less inventive, our goods and services no less needed than they were last week, or last month, or last year. Our capacity remains undiminished. But our time of standing pat, of protecting narrow interests and putting off unpleasant decisions—that time has surely passed. Starting today, we must pick ourselves up, dust ourselves off, and begin again the work of remaking America.

For everywhere we look, there is work to be done. The state of our economy calls for action, bold and swift. And we will act, not only to create new jobs, but to lay a new foundation for growth. We will build the roads and bridges, the electric grids and digital lines that feed our commerce and bind us together. We'll restore science to its rightful place and wield technology's wonders to raise health care's quality and lower its cost. We will harness the sun, and the winds, and the soil to fuel our cars and run our factories. And we will transform our schools and colleges and universities to meet the demands of a new age. All this we can do. All this we will do.

Now, there are some who question the scale of our ambitions, who suggest that our system cannot tolerate too many big plans. Their memories are short, for they have forgotten what this country has already done, what free men and women can achieve when imagination is joined to common purpose, and necessity to courage. What the cynics fail to understand is that the ground has shifted beneath them, that the stale political arguments that have consumed us for so long no longer apply.

The question we ask today is not whether our government is too big or too small, but whether it works—whether it helps families find jobs at a decent wage, care they can afford, a retirement that is dignified. Where the answer is yes, we intend to move forward. Where the answer is no, programs will end. And those of us who manage the public's dollars will be held to account, to spend wisely, reform bad habits, and do our business in the light of day, because only then can we restore the vital trust between a people and their government.

Nor is the question before us whether the market is a force for good or ill. Its power to generate wealth and expand freedom is unmatched. But this crisis has reminded us that without a watchful eye, the market can spin out of control. The nation cannot prosper long when it favors only the prosperous. The success of our economy has always depended not just on the size of our gross domestic product, but on the reach of our prosperity, on the ability to extend opportunity to every willing heart—not out of charity, but because it is the surest route to our common good.

As for our common defense, we reject as false the choice between our safety and our ideals. Our Founding Fathers, faced with perils that we can scarcely imagine, drafted a charter to assure the rule of law and the rights of man—a charter expanded by the blood of generations. Those ideals still light the world, and we will not give them up for expedience sake.

And so, to all the other peoples and governments who are watching today, from the grandest capitals to the small village where my father was born, know that America is a friend of each nation, and every man, woman, and child who seeks a future of peace and dignity. And we are ready to lead once more.

Recall that earlier generations faced down fascism and communism not just with missiles and tanks, but with the sturdy alliances and enduring convictions. They understood that our power alone cannot protect us, nor does it entitle us to do as we please. Instead, they knew that our power grows through its prudent use; our security emanates from the justness of our cause, the force of our example, the tempering qualities of humility and restraint.

We are the keepers of this legacy. Guided by these principles once more we can meet those new threats that demand even greater effort, even greater cooperation and understanding between nations. We will begin to responsibly leave Iraq to its people and forge a hard-earned peace in Afghanistan. With old friends and former foes, we'll work tirelessly to lessen the nuclear threat, and roll back the specter of a warming planet.

We will not apologize for our way of life, nor will we waver in its defense. And for those who seek to advance their aims by inducing terror and slaughtering innocents, we say to you now that our spirit is stronger and cannot be broken—you cannot outlast us, and we will defeat you.

For we know that our patchwork heritage is a strength, not a weakness. We are a nation of Christians and Muslims, Jews and Hindus, and non-believers. We are shaped by every language and culture, drawn from every end of this Earth; and because we have tasted the bitter swill of civil war and segregation, and emerged from that dark chapter stronger and more united, we cannot help but believe that the old hatreds shall someday pass; that the lines of tribe shall soon dissolve; that as the world grows smaller, our common humanity shall reveal itself; and that America must play its role in ushering in a new era of peace.

To the Muslim world, we seek a new way forward, based on mutual interest and mutual respect. To those leaders around the globe who seek to sow conflict, or blame their society's ills on the West, know that your people will judge you on what you can build, not what you destroy.

To those who cling to power through corruption and deceit and the silencing of dissent, know that you are on the wrong side of history, but that we will extend a hand if you are willing to unclench your fist.

To the people of poor nations, we pledge to work alongside you to make your farms flourish and let clean waters flow; to nourish starved bodies and feed hungry minds. And to those nations like ours that enjoy relative plenty, we say we can no longer afford indifference to the suffering outside our borders, nor can we consume the world's resources without regard to effect. For the world has changed, and we must change with it.

As we consider the role that unfolds before us, we remember with humble gratitude those brave Americans who at this very hour patrol far-off deserts and distant mountains. They have something to tell us, just as the fallen heroes who lie in Arlington whisper through the ages.

We honor them not only because they are the guardians of our liberty, but because they embody the spirit of service—a willingness to find meaning in something greater than themselves.

And yet at this moment, a moment that will define a generation, it is precisely this spirit that must inhabit us all. For as much as government can do, and must do, it is ultimately the faith and determination of the American people upon which this nation relies. It is the kindness to take in a stranger when the levees break, the selflessness of workers who would rather cut their hours than see a friend lose their job which sees us through our darkest hours. It is the firefighter's courage to storm a stairway filled with smoke, but also a parent's willingness to nurture a child that finally decides our fate.

Our challenges may be new. The instruments with which we meet them may be new. But those values upon which our success depends—honesty and hard work, courage and fair play, tolerance and curiosity, loyalty and patriotism—these things are old. These things are true. They have been the quiet force of progress throughout our history.

What is demanded, then, is a return to these truths. What is required of us now is a new era of responsibility—a recognition on the part of every American that we have duties to ourselves, our nation and the world; duties that we do not grudgingly accept, but rather seize gladly, firm in the knowledge that there is nothing so satisfying to the spirit, so defining of our character than giving our all to a difficult task.

This is the price and the promise of citizenship. This is the source of our confidence—the knowledge that God calls on us to shape an uncertain destiny. This is the meaning of our liberty and our creed, why men and women and children of every race and every faith can join in celebration across this magnificent mall; and why a man whose father less than sixty years ago might not have been served in a local restaurant can now stand before you to take a most sacred oath.

So let us mark this day with remembrance of who we are and how far we have traveled. In the year of America's birth, in the coldest of months, a small band of patriots huddled by dying campfires on the shores of an icy river. The capital was abandoned. The enemy was advancing. The snow was stained with blood. At the moment when the outcome of our revolution was most in doubt, the father of our nation ordered these words to be read to the people:

> *Let it be told to the future world . . . that in the depth of winter, when nothing but hope and virtue could survive . . . that the city and the country, alarmed at one common danger, came forth to meet [it].*

America: In the face of our common dangers, in this winter of our hardship, let us remember these timeless words. With hope and virtue, let us brave once more the icy currents, and endure what storms may come. Let it be said by our children's children that when we were tested, we refused to let this journey end, that we did not turn back nor did we falter; and with eyes fixed on the horizon and God's grace upon us, we carried forth that great gift of freedom and delivered it safely to future generations.

Thank you. God bless you. And God bless the United States of America.

CHAPTER 7

Barack Obama

The Global Financial Crisis and the American Recovery and Reinvestment Act

2009

It will not be easy. But if we move forward with purpose and resolve—with a deepened appreciation of how fundamental the American Dream is and how fragile it can be when we fail to live up to our collective responsibilities, if we go back to our roots, our core values, I am absolutely confident we will overcome this crisis and once again secure that dream not just for ourselves but for generations to come.

The American economy was in freefall from 2007 to 2009. The unemployment rate doubled from 5 percent to 10 percent, credit markets were frozen, Lehman Brothers filed for bankruptcy, and the economy was in its most severe contraction since World War II. Matters normally covered in the financial press became headlines in mainstream newspapers and on cable news.

While there was undoubtedly a crisis on Wall Street, the pain was being felt by Main Street, particularly the millions of homeowners who were facing the threat of eviction and losing their life savings as they defaulted on mortgages they could no longer afford.

One of the foundations of the American Dream is homeownership. The traditional social contract is that through working during your productive wage-earning years, Americans should be able to put a down payment on a house, take out an affordable mortgage, and then pay off the balance near retirement, at which point the equity in your home is yours to keep.

Aside from the economic merits, homeownership is positive for society in many ways. People feel invested in their homes and neighborhoods and care about their communities when they will be there for a long time. Social networks form at schools, parks, and religious organizations, improving the quality of people's lives.

President Obama came to office in January 2009 as the global financial crisis was devastating the lives of Americans, destroying the traditional aspect of the homeownership compact for many. The seeds of the crisis had been years in the making and started under prior administrations. Part of the reason Obama won the 2008 election was because he showed empathy for the average American, instilling a sense that Washington cared about people, and that rather than letting markets solve their own problems, the federal government could intervene to help.

Obama's speech commemorating the passage of the American Recovery and Reinvestment Act (ARRA) spoke to the hardships many families faced. It was controversial at the time because some saw it as strong-handed government intervention, simultaneously bailing out homeowners, banks, and the credit markets via the Federal Reserve's balance sheet, but at the end of the day, it worked. Millions of homeowners had their loans modified such that they could avoid foreclosure and maintain their life savings. Despite the large initial price tag—over $800 billion—by the time the nation emerged from the financial crisis, the government actually made money on the pro-grams it put in place. This was not the intended goal but dampened criticism by some Republicans who considered it a bailout for private individuals. The ARRA helped heal the U.S. economy while saving millions of people from homelessness, created policies that allowed markets to recover, restored liquidity to the financial system, and unleashed a decade of economic expansion.

This speech is notable not only because of the occasion, but because it frames complex issues in terms the average person can understand and shows empathy, foresight, and decisive leadership, rallying the power of the federal government with tremendous coor-dination between the public and private sectors. More recent politi-cal speeches tend not to show empathy. They place blame on the opposing political party and frame economic issues solely about taxes or earning points against foes. President Obama does none of these things.

In this speech, Obama talks about where the American Dream has failed and how he will use the power of the presidency to improve the lives of the average American at no cost to taxpayers. Obama acted in a bipartisan manner with policies that benefited both those who voted for and against him. His actions helped restore stabil-ity in America's housing markets and faith in the economy. It was a net positive for banks and those whose homes were not at direct risk of foreclosure. By addressing the crisis in a nonpartisan manner, Obama's words speak to the collective good and the missing center.

I'm here today to talk about a crisis unlike any we've ever known—but one that you know very well here in Mesa, and throughout the Valley. In Phoenix and its surround-ing suburbs, the American Dream is being tested by a home mortgage crisis that not only threatens the stability of our economy, but also the stability of families and neighborhoods. It's a crisis that strikes at the heart of the middle class: the homes in which we invest our savings and build our lives, raise our families, and plant roots in our communities.

So many Americans have shared with me their personal experiences of this crisis. Many have written letters or emails or shared their stories with me at rallies and along rope lines. Their hardship and heartbreak are a reminder that while this crisis is vast, it begins just one house—and one family—at a time.

It begins with a young family—maybe in Mesa, or Glendale, or Tempe—or just as likely in a suburban area of Las Vegas, or Cleveland, or Miami. They save up. They search. They choose a home that feels like the perfect place to start a life. They secure a fixed-rate mortgage at a reasonable rate, and they make a down payment, and they make their mortgage payments each month. They are as responsible as anyone could ask them to be.

But then they learn that acting responsibly often isn't enough to escape this crisis. Perhaps somebody loses a job in the latest round of layoffs, one of more than 3.5 million jobs lost since this recession began—or maybe a child gets sick, or a spouse has his or her hours cut.

In the past, if you found yourself in a situation like this, you could have sold your home and bought a smaller one with more affordable payments, or you could have refinanced your home at a lower rate. But today, home values have fallen so sharply that even if you make a large down payment, the current value of your mortgage may still be higher than the current value of your house. So, no bank will return your calls, and no sale will return your investment.

You can't afford to leave; you can't afford to stay. So, you start cutting back on luxuries. Then you start cutting back on necessities. You spend down your savings to keep up with your payments. Then you open the retirement fund. Then you use the credit cards. And when you've gone through everything you have, and done everything you can, you have no choice but to default on your loan. And so, your home joins the nearly six million others in foreclosure or at risk of foreclosure across the country, including roughly 150,000 right here in Arizona.

But the foreclosures which are uprooting families and upending lives across America are only part of the housing crisis. For while there are millions of families who face foreclosure, there are millions more who are in no danger of losing their homes, but who have still seen their dreams endangered. They're the families who see the 'For Sale' signs lining the streets; who see neighbors leave, and homes standing vacant, and lawns slowly turning brown. They see their own homes—their single largest asset—plummeting in value. One study in Chicago found that a foreclosed home reduces the price of nearby homes by as much as 9 percent. Home prices in cities across the country have fallen by more than 25 percent since 2006. And, in Phoenix, they've fallen by 43 percent.

Even if your neighborhood hasn't been hit by foreclosures, you're likely feeling the effects of this crisis in other ways. Companies in your community that depend on the housing market—construction companies and home furnishing stores and painters and landscapers—they're all cutting back and laying people off. The number of residential construction jobs has fallen by more than a quarter million since mid-2006. As businesses lose revenue and people lose income, the tax base shrinks, which means less money for schools and police and fire departments. And on top of this, the costs to local government associated with a single foreclosure can be as high as $20,000.

So, the effects of this crisis have also reverberated across the financial markets. When the housing market collapsed, so did the availability of credit on which our economy depends. And as that credit has dried up, it's been harder for families to find affordable loans to purchase a car or pay tuition, and harder for businesses to secure the capital they need to expand and create jobs.

In the end, all of us are paying a price for this home mortgage crisis. And all of us will pay an even steeper price if we allow this crisis to continue to deepen—a crisis which is unraveling homeownership, the middle class, and the American Dream itself. But if we act boldly and swiftly to arrest this downward spiral, then every American will benefit. And that's what I want to talk about today.

The plan I'm announcing focuses on rescuing families who've played by the rules and acted responsibly, by refinancing loans for millions of families in traditional mortgages who are underwater or close to it, by modifying loans for families stuck in subprime mortgages they can't afford as a result of skyrocketing interest rates or personal misfortune, and by taking broader steps to keep mortgage rates low so that families can secure loans with affordable monthly payments.

At the same time, this plan must be viewed in a larger context. A lost home often begins with a lost job. Many businesses have laid off workers for a lack of revenue and available capital. Credit has become scarce as markets have been overwhelmed by the collapse of securities backed by failing mortgages. In the end, the home mortgage crisis, the financial crisis, and this broader economic crisis are all interconnected, and we can't successfully address any one of them without addressing them all.

So yesterday, in Denver, I signed into law the American Recovery and Reinvestment Act, which will create or save 3.5 million jobs over the next two years—including 70,000 right here in Arizona—doing the work America needs done. And we're also going to work to stabilize, repair, and reform our financial system to get credit flowing again to families and businesses.

And we will pursue the housing plan I'm outlining today. And through this plan, we will help between seven and nine million families restructure or refinance their mortgages so they can avoid foreclosure. And we're not just helping homeowners at risk of falling over the edge; we're preventing their neighbors from being pulled over that edge too—as defaults and foreclosures contribute to sinking home values, failing local businesses, and lost jobs.

But I want to be very clear about what this plan will not do: it will not rescue the unscrupulous or irresponsible by throwing good taxpayer money after bad loans. It will not help speculators who took risky bets on a rising market and bought homes not to live in but to sell. It will not help dishonest lenders who acted irresponsibly, distorting the facts and dismissing the fine print at the expense of buyers who didn't know better. And it will not reward folks who bought homes they knew from the beginning they would never be able to afford. So, I just want to make this clear: This plan will not save every home.

But it will give millions of families resigned to financial ruin a chance to rebuild. It will prevent the worst consequences of this crisis from wreaking even greater havoc on the economy. And by bringing down the foreclosure rate, it will help to shore up housing prices for everybody.

According to estimates by the Treasury Department, this plan could stop the slide in home prices due to neighboring foreclosures by up to $6,000 per home.

So, here's how my plan works: First, we will make it possible for an estimated four to five million currently ineligible homeowners who receive their mortgages through Fannie Mae or Freddie Mac to refinance their mortgages at a lower rate.

Today, as a result of declining home values, millions of families are what's called "underwater," which simply means that they owe more on their mortgages than their homes are currently worth. These families are unable to sell their homes, but they're also unable to refinance them. So, in the event of a job loss or another emergency, their options are limited.

Also right now, Fannie Mae and Freddie Mac—the institutions that guarantee home loans for millions of middle-class families—are generally not permitted to guarantee refinancing for mortgages valued at more than 80 percent of the home's worth. So, families who are underwater or close to being underwater can't turn to these lending institutions for help.

My plan changes that by removing this restriction on Fannie and Freddie so that they can refinance mortgages they already own or guarantee.

And what this will do is it will allow millions of families stuck with loans at a higher rate to refinance. And the estimated cost to taxpayers would be roughly zero. While Fannie and Freddie would receive less money in payments, this would be balanced out by a reduction in defaults and foreclosures.

I also want to point out that millions of other households could benefit from historically low interest rates if they refinance, though many don't know that this opportunity is available to them—an opportunity that could save families hundreds of dollars each month. And the efforts we are taking to stabilize mortgage markets will help borrowers secure more affordable terms, too.

A second thing we're going to do under this plan is we will create new incentives so that lenders work with borrowers to modify the terms of subprime loans at risk of default and foreclosure.

Subprime loans—loans with high rates and complex terms that often conceal their costs—make up only 12 percent of all mortgages, but account for roughly half of all foreclosures. Right now, when families with these mortgages seek to modify a loan to avoid this fate, they often find themselves navigating a maze of rules and regulations, but they're rarely finding answers. Some subprime lenders are willing to renegotiate; but many aren't. And your ability to restructure your loan depends on where you live, the company that owns or manages your loan, or even the agent who happens to answer the phone on the day that you call.

So, here's what my plan does: [It] establishes clear guidelines for the entire mortgage industry that will encourage lenders to modify mortgages on primary residences. Any institution that wishes to receive financial assistance from the government, from taxpayers, and to modify home mortgages, will have to do so according to these guidelines—which will be in place two weeks from today.

Here's what this means: if lenders and home buyers work together, and the lender agrees to offer rates that the borrower can afford, then we'll make up part of the gap between what the old payments were and what the new payments will be. Under this plan, lenders who participate will be required to reduce those payments to no more than 31 percent of a borrower's income. And this will enable as many as three to four million homeowners to modify the terms of their mortgages to avoid foreclosure.

So, this part of the plan will require both buyers and lenders to step up and do their part, to take on some responsibility. Lenders will need to lower interest rates and share in the costs of reducing monthly payments in order to prevent another wave of foreclosures. Borrowers will be required to make payments on time in return for this opportunity to reduce those payments.

And I also want to be clear that there will be a cost associated with this plan. But by making these investments in foreclosure prevention today, we will save ourselves the costs of foreclosure tomorrow—costs that are borne not just by families with troubled loans, but by their neighbors and communities and by our economy as a whole. Given the magnitude of these crises, it is a price well worth paying.

There's a third part of the plan: We will take major steps to keep mortgage rates low for millions of middle-class families looking to secure new mortgages.

Today, most new home loans are backed by Fannie Mae and Freddie Mac, which guarantee loans and set standards to keep mortgage rates low and to keep mortgage financing available and predictable for middle-class families. Now, this function is profoundly important, especially now as we grapple with a crisis that would only worsen if we were to allow further disruptions in our mortgage markets.

Therefore, using the funds already approved by Congress for this purpose, the Treasury Department and the Federal

Reserve will continue to purchase Fannie Mae and Freddie Mac mortgage-backed securities so that there is stability and liquidity in the marketplace. Through its existing authority, [the] Treasury will provide up to $200 billion in capital to ensure that Fannie Mae and Freddie Mac can continue to stabilize markets and hold mortgage rates down.

And we're also going to work with Fannie and Freddie on other strategies to bolster the mortgage markets, like working with state housing finance agencies to increase their liquidity. And as we seek to ensure that these institutions continue to perform what is a vital function on behalf of middle-class families, we also need to maintain transparency and strong oversight so that they do so in responsible and effective ways.

Fourth, we will pursue a wide range of reforms designed to help families stay in their homes and avoid foreclosures.

And my administration will continue to support reforming our bankruptcy rules so that we allow judges to reduce home mortgages on primary residences to their fair market value—as long as borrowers pay their debts under court-ordered plans. I just want everybody to understand, that's the rule for investors who own two, three, and four homes. So it should be the rule for folks who just own one home as an alternative to foreclosure.

In addition, as part of the recovery plan I signed into law yesterday, we are going to award $2 billion in competitive grants to communities that are bringing together stakeholders and testing new and innovative ways to limit the effects of foreclosures. Communities have shown a lot of initiative, taking responsibility for this crisis when many others have not. And supporting these neighborhood efforts is exactly what we should be doing.

So taken together, the provisions of this plan will help us end this crisis and preserve for millions of families their stake in the American Dream. But we also have to acknowledge the limits of this plan.

Our housing crisis was born of eroding home values, but it was also an erosion of our common values, and in some case, common sense. It was brought about by big banks that traded in risky mortgages in return for profits that were literally too good to be true; by lenders who knowingly took advantage of homebuyers; by homebuyers who knowingly borrowed too much from lenders; by speculators who gambled on ever-rising prices; and by leaders in our nation's capital who failed to act amidst a deepening crisis.

So, solving this crisis will require more than resources; it will require all of us to step back and take responsibility. Government has to take responsibility for setting rules of the road that are fair and fairly enforced. Banks and lenders must be held accountable for ending the practices that got us into this crisis in the first place. And each of us, as individuals, have to take responsibility for their own actions. That means all of us have to learn to live within our means again and not assume that housing prices are going to go up 20, 30, 40 percent every year.

Those core values of common sense and responsibility, those are the values that have defined this nation. Those are the values that have given substance to our faith in the American Dream. Those are the values we have to restore now at this defining moment.

It will not be easy. But if we move forward with purpose and resolve—with a deepened appreciation of how fundamental the American Dream is and how fragile it can be when we fail to live up to our collective responsibilities, if we go back to our roots, our core values, I am absolutely confident we will overcome this crisis and once again secure that dream not just for ourselves but for generations to come.

Thank you. God bless you. God bless the United States of America.

CHAPTER 8

Hillary Clinton

United Nations Commission
on the Status of Women

2010

So we must measure our progress not by what we say in great venues like this, but in how well we are able to improve the condition of women's lives, some near at hand who deserve the opportunities many of us take for granted, some in far distant cities and remote villages—women we are not likely ever to meet but whose lives will be shaped by our actions.

H illary Clinton is one of the most well-recognized female American politicians of the modern era. After serving as the First Lady, she was elected as a U.S. senator representing New York. She was later appointed secretary of state under President Obama and ran for president in 2016—the first woman to lead a major U.S. party's presidential ticket. Clinton won the popular vote in the 2016 campaign against the Republican candidate Donald Trump but lost in the Electoral College.

It is ironic that gender is a major topic in U.S. politics. In peer nations, women have held leadership positions for decades. The United Kingdom elected Margaret Thatcher as their first female prime minister in 1979; Mary McAleese was elected president of Ireland in 1997; Germany's chancellor Angela Merkel was elected to office in 2005. These women have been widely recognized as successful leaders, yet America had never had a female commander in chief.

Hillary Clinton delivered the speech that is the subject of this chapter to the United Nations Commission on the Status of Women in March 2010, when she was the secretary of state. She speaks to the challenges women face around the world: inequalities in education, pay, and outcomes, as well as the failure of certain governments and cultures to protect their female citizens. This speech highlights the progress women have made while calling attention to the issues women still face.

Clinton's speech speaks to values that many American readers would consider basic and fundamental. Equal access to education and jobs and protection from abuse were codified in U.S. law long before 2010, but as Clinton's own experience demonstrates, they are still not always fully practiced today. Secretary Clinton calls upon the United States and the world, regardless of each nation's culture and religion, to respect female rights as equal rights.

This speech was bipartisan in the sense that it does not speak to political parties; it projected societal (albeit Western) values on the need to protect human rights—rights which to an American reader seem fundamental but to certain other cultures and societies may not be. Her speech succeeded by thrusting this issue onto the world stage. For those who might have had a different perspective, she exhibited qualities we see in other great speeches to change hearts and minds. She won over her audience by citing humane examples paired with a call to action and a commitment to the collective ideal that women's rights are a part of the fundamental compact of human rights to which every nation in the U.N. must be accountable.

———————

Thank you. Thank you to Ambassador Alex Wolff and to our U.S. Mission here at the United Nations. And it's wonderful to be back at the United Nations for this occasion.

. . . This final day of the 54th session of the U.N. Commission brings to a close a week of a lot of activity, and it reminds us of the work that still lies ahead.

Fifteen years ago, delegates from 189 countries met in Beijing for the Fourth World Conference on Women. It was a call to action—a call to the global community to work for the laws, reforms, and social changes necessary to ensure that women and girls everywhere finally have the opportunities they deserve to fulfill their own God-given potentials and contribute fully to the progress and prosperity of their societies.

For many of us in this room today, that was a call to action that we have heeded. I know some of you have made it the cause of your life. You have worked tirelessly, day in and day out, to translate those words into realities. And we have seen the evidence of such efforts everywhere.

In South Africa, women living in shanty towns came together to build a housing development outside Cape Town all on their own, brick by brick. And today, their community has grown to more than fifty thousand homes for low-income families, most of them female-headed.

In Liberia, a group of church women began a prayer movement to stop their country's brutal civil war. It grew to include thousands of women who helped force the two sides to negotiate a peace agreement. And then, those women helped elect Ellen Johnson Sirleaf president, the first woman to lead an African nation.

In the United States, a young woman had an idea for a website where anyone could help a small business on the other side of the world get off the ground. And today, the organization she co-founded, Kiva, has given more than $120 million in microloans to entrepreneurs in developing countries, 80 percent of them women.

So, as we meet here in New York, women worldwide are working hard to do their part to improve the status of women and girls. And in so doing, they are also improving the status of families, communities, and countries. They are running domestic violence shelters and fighting human trafficking. They are rescuing girls from brothels in Cambodia and campaigning for public office in Kuwait. They are healing women injured in childbirth in Ethiopia, providing legal aid to women in China, and running schools for refugees from Burma. They are rebuilding homes and re-stitching communities in the aftermath of the earthquakes in Haiti and Chile. And they are literally leaving their marks on the world. For example, thanks to the environmental movement started by Nobel Laureate Wangari Maathai, 45 million trees are now standing tall across Kenya, most of them planted by women.

And even young girls have been empowered to stand up for their rights in ways that were once unthinkable. In Yemen, a ten-year-old girl forced to marry a much older man made headlines around the world by marching into court and demanding that she be granted a divorce, which she received. And her courage helped to shine a spotlight on the continuing practice of child marriage in that country and elsewhere.

Now, these are just a few of the stories, and everyone here could stand up and tell even more. These are the stories of what women around the world do every day to confront injustice, to solve crises, propel economies, improve living conditions, and promote peace. Women have shown time and again that they will seize opportunities to improve their own and their families' lives. And even when it seems that no opportunity exists, they still find a way. And thanks to the hard work and persistence of women and men, we have made real gains toward meeting the goals set in Beijing.

Today, more girls are in school. More women hold jobs and serve in public office. And as women have gained the chance to work, learn, and participate in their societies, their economic, political, and social contributions have multiplied. In many countries, laws that once permitted the unequal treatment of women have been replaced by laws that recognize their equality, although for too many, laws that exist on the books are not yet borne out in their daily lives.

But the progress we have made in the past fifteen years is by no means the end of the story. It is, maybe, if we're really lucky, the end of the beginning. There is still so much more to be done. We have to write the next chapter to fully realize the dreams and potential that we set forth in Beijing. Because for too many millions and millions of girls and women, opportunity remains out of reach. Women are still the majority of the world's poor, the uneducated, the unhealthy, the unfed. In too many places, women are treated not as full and equal human beings with their own rights and aspirations, but as lesser creatures undeserving of the treatment and respect accorded to their husbands, their fathers, and their sons.

Women are the majority of the world's farmers but are often forbidden from owning the land they tend to every day, or accessing the credit they need to invest in those farms and make them more productive.

Women care for the world's sick, but women and girls are less likely to get treatment when they are sick.

Women raise the world's children, but too often receive inadequate care when they give birth. And as a result, childbirth remains a leading cause of death and injury to women worldwide.

Women rarely cause armed conflicts, but they always suffer their consequences. And when warring sides sit at one table to negotiate peace, women are often excluded, even though it is their future and their children's future that is being decided.

Though many countries have passed laws to deter violence against women, it remains a global pandemic. Women and girls are bought and sold to settle debts and resolve disputes. They are raped as both a tactic and a prize of armed conflict. They are beaten as punishment for disobedience and as a warning to other women who might assert their rights. And millions of women and girls are enslaved in brothels, forced to work as prostitutes, while police officers pocket bribes and look the other way.

Women may be particularly vulnerable to human rights violations like these. But we also know that in many places, women now are leading the fight to protect and promote human rights for everyone. With us today are several women I was proud to honor earlier this week at this year's United States State Department's International Women of Courage Awards. They have endured isolation and intimidation, violence and imprisonment, and even risked their lives to advance justice and freedom for others. And though they may work in lonely circumstances, these women, and those like them around the world, are not alone. Let them know that every one of us and the many others whom we represent are standing with them as they wage their lonely but essential efforts on behalf of us all.

The status of the world's women is not only a matter of morality and justice. It is also a political, economic, and social imperative. Put simply, the world cannot make lasting progress if women and girls in the twenty-first century are denied their rights and left behind.

The other day I heard *The New York Times* columnist Nick Kristof, who has done so much to bring to a wide audience the stories of individual women who are working and suffering because of conditions under which they are oppressed. And he said in the nineteenth century, the great moral imperative was the fight against slavery. And in the twentieth century, it was the fight against totalitarianism. And in the twenty-first century, it is the fight for women's equality. He was right, and we must accept—and promote that fundamental truth.

Now, I know there are those—hard to believe—but there are those who still dispute the importance of women to local, national, and global progress. But the evidence is irrefutable. When women are free to develop their talents, all people benefit: women and men, girls and boys. When women are free to vote and run for public office, governments are more effective and responsive to their people. When women are free to earn a living and start small businesses, the data is clear: They become key drivers of economic growth across regions and sectors. When women are given the opportunity of education and access to health care, their families and communities prosper.

And when women have equal rights, nations are more stable, peaceful, and secure.

In 1995, in one voice, the world declared human rights are women's rights and women's rights are human rights. And for many, those words have translated into concrete actions. But for others they remain a distant aspiration. Change on a global scale cannot and does not happen overnight. It takes time, patience, and persistence. And as hard as we have worked these past fifteen years, we have more work to do.

So today, let us renew our commitment to finishing the job. And let us intensify our efforts because it is both the right thing to do, and it is the smart thing as well. We must declare with one voice that women's progress is human progress, and human progress is women's progress, once and for all.

This principle was enshrined ten years ago in Millennium Development Goal Number 3, the promotion of gender equality and the empowerment of women. And that goal is essential for the realization of every other goal. Today, this principle is also at the heart of the foreign policy of the United States. We believe that women are critical to solving virtually every challenge we face as individual nations and as a community of nations. Strategies that ignore the lives and contributions of women have little chance of succeeding. So, in the Obama administration, we are integrating women throughout our work around the world.

We are consulting with women as we design and implement our policies. We are taking into greater account how those policies will impact women and girls. And we are working to identify women leaders and potential leaders around the world to make them our partners and to help support their work. And we are measuring progress, in part, by how much we improve the conditions of the lives of women and girls.

This isn't window dressing, and it's not just good politics. President Obama and I believe that the subjugation of women is a threat to the national security of the United States. It is also a threat to the common security of our world, because the suffering and denial of the rights of women and the instability of nations go hand in hand.

The United States is implementing this approach in our strategy in Afghanistan. As I said in London in January at the International Conference on Afghanistan, the women of Afghanistan have to be involved at every step in securing and rebuilding their country. Our stabilization strategy for both Afghanistan and Pakistan includes a Women's Action Plan that promotes women's leadership in both the public and private sectors; increases their access to education, health, and justice; and generates jobs for women, especially in agriculture.

This focus on women has even been embraced by the United States military. All-women teams of Marines will be meeting with Afghan women in their homes to assess their needs. Congress has joined this focus as well. The Senate Foreign Relations Committee, under Chairman John Kerry, empowered a subcommittee charged with global women's issues that recently held hearings on promoting opportunity for Afghan women and girls.

History has taught us that any peace not built by and for women is far less likely to deliver real and lasting benefits. As we have seen from Guatemala to Northern Ireland to Bosnia, women can be powerful peacemakers, willing to reach across deep divides to find common ground. United Nations Security Council Resolution 1325 reflects this principle. Now, we must work together to render it into action and achieve the full participation of women as equal partners in peace. And as women continue to advocate for peace, even risking their lives to achieve it, many are praying that we will keep the promise we made in Resolution 1888 to take significant steps to end sexual violence against women and children in conflict.

We have begun the process laid out in the resolution. Secretary-General Ban Ki-moon has appointed a special representative. Now we must press ahead to end forever the evil of rape in conflict, which has caused suffering beyond imagination for victims and their families.

For the United States, women are also central to our ongoing work to elevate development as a key pillar of our foreign policy alongside diplomacy and defense. As those who grow the world's food, collect the water, gather the firewood, wash the clothes, and increasingly, work in the factories, run the shops, launch the businesses, and create jobs, women are powerful forces for any country's economic growth and social progress. So, our development strategies must reflect their roles and the benefits they bring.

Three major foreign policy initiatives illustrate our commitment. The first is our Global Health Initiative, a $63 billion commitment to improve health and strengthen health systems worldwide. Improving global health is an enormous undertaking, so we are focusing first on those people whose health has the biggest impact on families and communities, women and girls. We aim to reduce maternal and child mortality and increase access to family planning. And we especially commend the commission and the U.N.'s adoption by consensus of the resolution on maternal mortality.

We also intend to further reduce the numbers of new HIV infections. AIDS has now become a woman's disease, passed from men to women and too often, to children. Through our Global Health Initiative and our continued work through PEPFAR, we hope to stop that deadly progression by giving women and girls the tools and knowledge they need to protect themselves, and by treating HIV-positive mothers so they are less likely to pass on the disease to their children.

Our global food security program, which I previewed here at the United Nations last September, is a $3.5 billion commitment to strengthen the world's food supply, so farmers can earn enough to support their families and food can be available more broadly. And women are integral to this mission. Most of the world's food is grown, harvested, stored, and prepared by women, often in extremely difficult conditions. They face droughts, floods, storms, pests without the fertilizers or enriched seeds that farmers in wealthy countries use. Many consider themselves lucky if they can scratch out a harvest sufficient to feed their children. Giving these women the tools and the training to grow more food and the opportunity to get that food to a market where it can be sold will have a transformative impact on their lives and it will grow the economies of so many countries.

I have to confess that when we started our Food Security Initiative, I did not know that most food was grown by women. I remember once driving through Africa with a group of distinguished experts. And I saw women working in the fields and I saw women working in the markets and I saw women with wood on their heads and water on their heads and children on their backs. And I remarked that women just seem to be working all the time. And one of the economists said, "But it doesn't count." I said, "How can you say that?" He said, "Well, it's not part of the formal economy." I said, "Well, if every woman who did all that work stopped tomorrow, the formal economy would collapse."

A third initiative is our government's response to the challenge of climate change. In Copenhagen in December, I announced that the United States would work with other countries to mobilize $100 billion a year by 2020 to address the climate needs of developing countries.

The effects of climate change will be felt by us all, but women in developing countries will be particularly hard hit, because as all of the changes of weather go on to produce more drought conditions and more storms and more floods, the women will have to work even harder to produce food and walk even farther to find water safe for drinking. They are on the front lines of this crisis, which makes them key partners and problem solvers. So we believe we must increase women's access to adaptation and mitigation technologies and programs so they can protect their families and help us all meet this global challenge.

These initiatives amount to more than an assortment of programs designed with women in mind. They reflect a fundamental shift in U.S. policy, one that is taking place in offices across Washington and in our embassies around the globe. But we are still called to do more—every single one of us. The Obama administration will continue to work for the ratification of CEDAW.

Now, I don't have to tell those of you who are Americans how hard this is. But we are determined, because we believe it is past time, to take this step for women in our country and in all countries. Here at the United Nations, a single, vibrant agency dedicated to women—run by a strong leader with a seat at the secretary-general's table, would help galvanize the greater levels of coordination and commitment that the women of the world deserve.

And as the United Nations strives to better support the world's women, it would benefit from having more women in more of its leadership positions. Just as there are talented women working unnoticed in every corner of the world, there are women with great talent and experience whose potential leadership is still largely untapped, and they deserve the chance to serve and lead.

The Beijing Declaration and the Platform for Action was not only a pledge to help women in other lands, it was also a promise by all countries to do more to advance opportunity and equality for our own citizens. Because in every country on earth, talent is universal, but opportunity is not. In my travels across the United States, I've met women for whom higher education is a distant dream. They have the talent, they have the drive, but they don't have the money. I've met mothers trapped in abusive relationships desperate to escape with their children, but with no means of support. I've met too many women who cannot afford necessary health care for themselves and their children. And I've met girls who have heard their whole lives that they were less than—less talented, less worthy of respect—until they eventually came to believe it was true.

So, whether we live in New York or New Delhi, Lagos or La Paz, women and girls share many of the same struggles and aspirations. The principle of women's equality is a simple, self-evident truth, but the work of turning that principle into practice is rarely simple. It takes years and even generations of patient, persistent work, not only to change a country's laws, but to change its people's minds, to weave throughout culture and tradition in public discourse and private views the unassailable fact of women's worth and women's rights.

Some of you may have seen the cover of the most recent issue of *The Economist*. If you haven't, I commend it to you. And like me, you may do a double take. Because I looked quickly at it and I thought it said "genocide." And then I looked more carefully at it, and it said "gendercide." Because it was pointing out the uncomfortable fact that there are approximately 100 million fewer girls than there should be, if one looked at all the population data. I was so struck by that: a word that I had never heard before, but which so tragically describes what has gone on, what we have let go on, in our world.

My daughter is here with me today—and being the mother of a daughter is a great inspiration and motivation for caring about the girls of the world. And I would hope that we would want not only for our own daughters the opportunities that we know would give them the chance to make the most of their lives, to fulfill that God-given potential that resides within each of us, but that we would recognize doing the same for other daughters of mothers and fathers everywhere would make the world a safer and better place for our own children.

So, we must measure our progress not by what we say in great venues like this, but in how well we are able to improve the condition of women's lives, some near at hand who deserve the opportunities many of us take for granted, some in far distant cities and remote villages—women we are not likely ever to meet but whose lives will be shaped by our actions.

Let us recommit ourselves, as individuals, as nations, as the United Nations, to build upon the progress of the past and achieve once and for all that principle that we all believe in, or we would not be here today. The rights and opportunities of all women and girls deserve our attention and our support because as they make progress, then the progress that should be the birthright of future generations will be more likely, and the twenty-first century will fulfill the promise that we hold out today. So, let's go forth and be reenergized in the work that lies ahead.

Thank you all very much.

CHAPTER 9

Barack Obama

The Death of Osama bin Laden

2011

The cause of securing our country is not complete. But tonight, we are once again reminded that America can do whatever we set our mind to. That is the story of our history, whether it's the pursuit of prosperity for our people, or the struggle for equality for all our citizens; our commitment to stand up for our values abroad, and our sacrifices to make the world a safer place.

The legacy of 9/11 continues to haunt the collective consciousness of Americans. Not since Pearl Harbor had there been a large-scale foreign attack on American soil. It changed people's perceptions of safety, redefined the notion of an enemy to include non-nation-state actors, and destroyed thousands of families. America entered a series of conflicts in the Middle East to root out the source of terror. While accomplishments were made in dismantling al Qaeda's ability to launch a repeat attack, the man who master-minded the atrocities was still on the loose.

On May 2, 2011, President Obama delivered a stirring address as commander in chief announcing that Osama bin Laden had been killed by an American military operation in Pakistan. Obama's speech was direct in his choice of words, nuanced in tone, and mas-terfully delivered. In a stunning oratory, he praised the heroism of the Navy SEALs, gave Americans a sense of justice, and honored the memories of the victims who lost their lives at the World Trade Center, at the Pentagon, and on commercial flights on September 11, including the first responders who died trying to save others.

Americans had been shaken post-9/11. Nearly ten years since the attack our troops had been on foreign soil fighting an elusive enemy. People wanted the mastermind of the attack held accountable. While there was debate whether American involvement in the Middle East was justified in scale, scope, and cost, Americans were unified in wanting to see bin Laden brought to justice.

Whether people agreed or disagreed with Obama's domestic and foreign policies, he rose above partisanship and talked to the entire nation in this rousing speech, which was notably devoid of mention of political parties. He went out of his way to make it clear that America's enemy was not the Muslim world, but the perpetrators who attacked innocent civilians. Obama spoke to the highest level of American values and the heroism of soldiers who put themselves in harm's way, delivering a poignant speech to help bring justice and healing from a terrorist attack.

Good evening. Tonight, I can report to the American people and to the world that the United States has con-ducted an operation that killed Osama bin Laden, the leader of al Qaeda, and a terrorist who's responsible for the murder of thousands of innocent men, women, and children.

It was nearly ten years ago that a bright September day was darkened by the worst attack on the American people in our history. The images of 9/11 are seared into our national memory—hijacked planes cutting through a cloudless September sky; the Twin Towers collapsing to the ground; black smoke billowing up from the Pentagon; the wreckage of Flight 93 in Shanksville, Pennsylvania, where the actions of heroic citizens saved even more heartbreak and destruction.

And yet we know that the worst images are those that were unseen to the world. The empty seat at the dinner table. Children who were forced to grow up without their mother or their father. Parents who would never know the feeling of their child's embrace. Nearly three thousand citizens taken from us, leaving a gaping hole in our hearts.

On September 11, 2001, in our time of grief, the American people came together. We offered our neighbors a hand, and we offered the wounded our blood. We reaffirmed our ties to each other, and our love of community and country. On that day, no matter where we came from, what God we prayed to, or what race or ethnicity we were, we were united as one American family.

We were also united in our resolve to protect our nation and to bring those who committed this vicious attack to justice. We quickly learned that the 9/11 attacks were carried out by al Qaeda—an organization headed by Osama bin Laden, which had openly declared war on the United States and was committed to killing innocents in our country and around the globe. And so we went to war against al Qaeda to protect our citizens, our friends, and our allies.

Over the last ten years, thanks to the tireless and heroic work of our military and our counterterrorism professionals, we've made great strides in that effort. We've disrupted terrorist attacks and strengthened our homeland defense. In Afghanistan, we removed the Taliban government, which had given bin Laden and al Qaeda safe haven and support. And around the globe, we worked with our friends and allies to capture or kill scores of al Qaeda terrorists, including several who were a part of the 9/11 plot.

Yet, Osama bin Laden avoided capture and escaped across the Afghan border into Pakistan. Meanwhile, al Qaeda continued to operate from along that border and operate through its affiliates across the world.

And so shortly after taking office, I directed Leon Panetta, the director of the CIA, to make the killing or capture of bin Laden the top priority of our war against al Qaeda, even as we continued our broader efforts to disrupt, dismantle, and defeat his network.

Then, last August, after years of painstaking work by our intelligence community, I was briefed on a possible lead to bin Laden. It was far from certain, and it took many months to run this thread to ground. I met repeatedly with my national security team as we developed more information about the possibility that we had located bin Laden hiding within a compound deep inside of Pakistan. And finally, last week, I determined that we had enough intelligence to take action and authorized an operation to get Osama bin Laden and bring him to justice.

Today, at my direction, the United States launched a targeted operation against that compound in Abbottabad, Pakistan. A small team of Americans carried out the operation with extraordinary courage and capability. No Americans were harmed. They took care to avoid civilian casualties. After a firefight, they killed Osama bin Laden and took custody of his body.

For over two decades, bin Laden has been al Qaeda's leader and symbol, and has continued to plot attacks against our country and our friends and allies. The death of bin Laden marks the most significant achievement to date in our nation's effort to defeat al Qaeda.

Yet his death does not mark the end of our effort. There's no doubt that al Qaeda will continue to pursue attacks against us. We must—and we will—remain vigilant at home and abroad.

As we do, we must also reaffirm that the United States is not—and never will be—at war with Islam. I've made clear, just as President Bush did shortly after 9/11, that our war is not against Islam. Bin Laden was not a Muslim leader; he was a mass murderer of Muslims. Indeed, al Qaeda has slaughtered scores of Muslims in many countries, including our own. So, his demise should be welcomed by all who believe in peace and human dignity.

Over the years, I've repeatedly made clear that we would take action within Pakistan if we knew where bin Laden was. That is what we've done. But it's important to note that our counterterrorism cooperation with Pakistan helped lead us to bin Laden and the compound where he was hiding. Indeed, bin Laden had declared war against Pakistan as well, and ordered attacks against the Pakistani people.

Tonight, I called President Zardari, and my team has also spoken with their Pakistani counterparts. They agree that this is a good and historic day for both of our nations. And going forward, it is essential that Pakistan continue to join us in the fight against al Qaeda and its affiliates.

The American people did not choose this fight. It came to our shores and started with the senseless slaughter of our citizens. After nearly ten years of service, struggle, and sacrifice, we know well the costs of war. These efforts weigh on me every time I, as commander in chief, have to sign a letter to a family that has lost a loved one, or look into the eyes of a service member who's been gravely wounded.

So, Americans understand the costs of war. Yet as a country, we will never tolerate our security being threatened, nor stand idly by when our people have been killed. We will be relentless in defense of our citizens and our friends and allies. We will be true to the values that make us who we are. And on nights like this one, we can say to those families who have lost loved ones to al Qaeda's terror: Justice has been done.

Tonight, we give thanks to the countless intelligence and counterterrorism professionals who've worked tirelessly to achieve this outcome. The American people do not see their work, nor know their names. But tonight, they feel the satisfaction of their work and the result of their pursuit of justice.

We give thanks for the men who carried out this operation, for they exemplify the professionalism, patriotism, and unparalleled courage of those who serve our country. And they are part of a generation that has borne the heaviest share of the burden since that September day.

Finally, let me say to the families who lost loved ones on 9/11 that we have never forgotten your loss, nor wavered in our commitment to see that we do whatever it takes to prevent another attack on our shores.

And tonight, let us think back to the sense of unity that prevailed on 9/11. I know that it has, at times, frayed. Yet today's achievement is a testament to the greatness of our country and the determination of the American people.

The cause of securing our country is not complete. But tonight, we are once again reminded that America can do whatever we set our mind to. That is the story of our history, whether it's the pursuit of prosperity for our people, or the struggle for equality for all our citizens; our commitment to stand up for our values abroad, and our sacrifices to make the world a safer place.

Let us remember that we can do these things not just because of wealth or power, but because of who we are: one nation, under God, indivisible, with liberty and justice for all.

Thank you. May God bless you. And may God bless the United States of America.

CHAPTER 10

Hillary Clinton

Human Rights are Gay Rights

2011

There is a phrase that people in the United States invoke when urging others to support human rights: "be on the right side of history." The story of the United States is the story of a nation that has repeatedly grappled with intolerance and inequality. We fought a brutal civil war over slavery. People from coast to coast joined in campaigns to recognize the rights of women, indigenous peoples, racial minorities, children, people with disabilities, immigrants, workers, and on and on. And the march toward equality and justice has continued.

For many younger Americans, LGBTQ+ rights are accepted and part of the norms in which they were raised. The Supreme Court ruled in favor of gay marriage in 2015 and public opinion supports it. Since roughly 2013, the majority of Americans have agreed that same-sex couples should have the same rights and recognition as other married couples.

In the United States, the law offers equal rights in health care, employee benefits, and self-determination regardless of one's sexuality. While some take these concepts to be self-evident, just like every evolution in what are considered fundamental civil rights, they were long fought for both in the United States and other places around the world before such protections became solidified in society and law.

Hillary Clinton brought significant attention to this matter on the global stage in a 2011 speech at the United Nations. At the time, America—along with most European democracies—had embraced gay rights and codified protections for the LGBTQ+ community into law. However, many parts of the world had yet to do this. Clinton used this speech to advocate for global protections for LGBTQ+ communities and implored nations who had not yet done so to evolve their definition of basic human rights.

Clinton's speech reminds us that everyone, regardless of who they love, should have equal protection no matter where they live. Knowing many in the audience would have dissenting views due to their nation's cultural or religious norms, Clinton goes to great lengths to emphasize that she is not trying to push Western values on others but rather to redefine universally held beliefs and protections. She appeals to compassion and humanity, arguing that our choice of who to love should not result in stigmatization, or being sentenced to prison or death.

This speech is notable because it avoids proclaiming Judeo-Christian values as superior. It directly addresses the concerns of the individual and the idea that all people should live in safety, be able to express their own views, and have access to food and medicine regardless of their sexuality. Clinton reminds the world that the United States' human rights record is not perfect and has evolved over the past two hundred years. In this rousing speech, she reminds the rest of the world that the choice of who one loves should be an equal, inalienable right in a well-delivered address touching on history, legal precedent, and heartfelt emotion to advocate for global standards on the issue.

Clinton's timing on the speech marked a watershed moment where support for gay marriage began to evolve to one of bipartisan consensus in the United States. Same-sex marriage had historically been favored by Democrats but was not widely embraced by Republicans. In a series of surveys conducted after the speech, Republican views started to shift and exactly ten years after the speech was delivered, a majority of Republicans agreed that same-sex marriage should be recognized by law. This speech helped set the stage for evolving views among Americans of both parties on political protections for same-sex marriage.

Good evening, and let me express my deep honor and pleasure at being here. I want to thank Director General Tokayev and Ms. Wyden along with other ministers, ambassadors, excellencies, and U.N. partners. This weekend, we will celebrate Human Rights Day, the anniversary of one of the great accomplishments of the last century.

Beginning in 1947, delegates from six continents devoted themselves to drafting a declaration that would enshrine the fundamental rights and freedoms of people everywhere. In the aftermath of World War II, many nations pressed for a statement of this kind to help ensure that we would prevent future atrocities and protect the inherent humanity and dignity of all people. And so the delegates went to work. They discussed, they wrote, they revisited, revised, rewrote, for thousands of hours. And they incorporated suggestions and revisions from governments, organizations, and individuals around the world.

At three o'clock in the morning on December 10th, 1948, after nearly two years of drafting and one last long night of debate, the president of the U.N. General Assembly called for a vote on the final text. Forty-eight nations voted in favor; eight abstained; none dissented. And the Universal Declaration of Human Rights was adopted. It proclaims a simple, powerful idea: All human beings are born free and equal in dignity and rights. And with the declaration, it was made clear that rights are not conferred by government; they are the birthright of all people. It does not matter what country we live in, who our leaders are, or even who we are. Because we are human, we therefore have rights. And because we have rights, governments are bound to protect them.

In the sixty-three years since the declaration was adopted, many nations have made great progress in making human rights a human reality. Step by step, barriers that once prevented people from enjoying the full measure of liberty, the full experience of dignity, and the full benefits of humanity have fallen away. In many places, racist laws have been repealed, legal and social practices that relegated women to second-class status have been abolished, the ability of religious minorities to practice their faith freely has been secured.

In most cases, this progress was not easily won. People fought and organized and campaigned in public squares and private spaces to change not only laws, but hearts and minds. And thanks to that work of generations, for millions of individuals whose lives were once narrowed by injustice, they are now able to live more freely and to participate more fully in the political, economic, and social lives of their communities.

Now, there is still, as you all know, much more to be done to secure that commitment, that reality, and progress for all people. Today, I want to talk about the work we have left to do to protect one group of people whose human rights are still denied in too many parts of the world today. In many ways, they are an invisible minority. They are arrested, beaten, terrorized, even executed. Many are treated with contempt and violence by their fellow citizens while authorities empowered to protect them look the other way or, too often, even join in the abuse. They are denied opportunities to work and learn, driven from their homes and countries, and forced to suppress or deny who they are to protect themselves from harm.

I am talking about gay, lesbian, bisexual, and transgender people, human beings born free and given bestowed equality and dignity, who have a right to claim that, which is now one of the remaining human rights challenges of our time. I speak about this subject knowing that my own country's record on human rights for gay people is far from perfect. Until 2003, it was still a crime in parts of our country. Many LGBT Americans have endured violence and harassment in their own lives, and for some, including many young people, bullying and exclusion are daily experiences. So we, like all nations, have more work to do to protect human rights at home.

Now, raising this issue, I know, is sensitive for many people and that the obstacles standing in the way of protecting the human rights of LGBT people rest on deeply held personal, political, cultural, and religious beliefs. So I come here before you with respect, understanding, and humility. Even though progress on this front is not easy, we cannot delay acting. So in that spirit, I want to talk about the difficult and important issues we must address together to reach a global consensus that recognizes the human rights of LGBT citizens everywhere.

The first issue goes to the heart of the matter. Some have suggested that gay rights and human rights are separate and distinct; but, in fact, they are one and the same. Now, of course, sixty years ago, the governments that drafted and passed the Universal Declaration of Human Rights were not thinking about how it applied to the LGBT community. They also weren't thinking about how it applied to indigenous people or children or people with disabilities or other marginalized groups. Yet in the past sixty years, we have come to recognize that members of these groups are entitled to the full measure of dignity and rights, because, like all people, they share a common humanity.

This recognition did not occur all at once. It evolved over time. And as it did, we understood that we were honoring rights that people always had, rather than creating new or special rights for them. Like being a woman, like being a racial, religious, tribal, or ethnic minority, being LGBT does not make you less human. And that is why gay rights are human rights, and human rights are gay rights.

It is violation of human rights when people are beaten or killed because of their sexual orientation, or because they do not conform to cultural norms about how men and women should look or behave. It is a violation of human rights when governments declare it illegal to be gay or allow those who harm gay people to go unpunished. It is a violation of human rights when lesbian or transgendered women are subjected to so-called corrective rape, or forcibly subjected to hormone treatments, or when people are murdered after public calls for violence toward gays, or when they are forced to flee their nations and seek asylum in other lands to save their lives. And it is a violation of human rights when life-saving care is withheld from people because they are gay, or equal access to justice is denied to people because they are gay, or public spaces are out of bounds to people because they are gay. No matter what we look like, where we come from, or who we are, we are all equally entitled to our human rights and dignity.

The second issue is a question of whether homosexuality arises from a particular part of the world. Some seem to believe it is a Western phenomenon, and therefore people outside the West have grounds to reject it. Well, in reality, gay people are born into and belong to every society in the world. They are all ages, all races, all faiths; they are doctors and teachers, farmers and bankers, soldiers and athletes; and whether we know it, or whether we acknowledge it, they are our family, our friends, and our neighbors.

Being gay is not a Western invention; it is a human reality. And protecting the human rights of all people, gay or straight, is not something that only Western governments do. South Africa's constitution, written in the aftermath of apartheid, protects the equality of all citizens, including gay people. In Colombia and Argentina, the rights of gays are also legally protected. In Nepal, the supreme court has ruled that equal rights apply to LGBT citizens. The government of Mongolia has committed to pursue new legislation that will tackle antigay discrimination.

Now, some worry that protecting the human rights of the LGBT community is a luxury that only wealthy nations can afford. But in fact, in all countries, there are costs to not protecting these rights, in both gay and straight lives lost to disease and violence, and the silencing of voices and views that would strengthen communities, in ideas never pursued by entrepreneurs who happen to be gay. Costs are incurred whenever any group is treated as lesser or the other, whether they are women, racial, or religious minorities, or the LGBT. Former president Mogae of Botswana pointed out recently that for as long as LGBT people are kept in the shadows, there cannot be an effective public health program to tackle HIV and AIDS. Well, that holds true for other challenges as well.

The third, and perhaps most challenging, issue arises when people cite religious or cultural values as a reason to violate or not to protect the human rights of LGBT citizens. This is not unlike the justification offered for violent practices towards women like honor killings, widow burning, or female genital mutilation. Some people still defend those practices as part of a cultural tradition. But violence toward women isn't cultural; it's criminal. Likewise with slavery, what was once justified as sanctioned by God is now properly reviled as an unconscionable violation of human rights.

In each of these cases, we came to learn that no practice or tradition trumps the human rights that belong to all of us. And this holds true for inflicting violence on LGBT people, criminalizing their status or behavior, expelling them from their families and communities, or tacitly or explicitly accepting their killing.

Of course, it bears noting that rarely are cultural and religious traditions and teachings actually in conflict with the protection of human rights. Indeed, our religion and our culture are sources of compassion and inspiration toward our fellow human beings. It was not only those who've justified slavery who leaned on religion, it was also those who sought to abolish it. And let us keep in mind that our commitments to protect the freedom of religion and to defend the dignity of LGBT people emanate from a common source. For many of us, religious belief and practice is a vital source of meaning and identity, and fundamental to who we are as people. And likewise, for most of us, the bonds of love and family that we forge are also vital sources of meaning and identity. And caring for others is an expression of what it means to be fully human. It is because the human experience is universal that human rights are universal and cut across all religions and cultures.

The fourth issue is what history teaches us about how we make progress towards rights for all. Progress starts with honest discussion. Now, there are some who say and believe that all gay people are pedophiles, that homosexuality is a disease that can be caught or cured, or that gays recruit others to become gay. Well, these notions are simply not true. They are also unlikely to disappear if those who promote or accept them are dismissed out of hand rather than invited to share their fears and concerns. No one has ever abandoned a belief because he was forced to do so.

Universal human rights include freedom of expression and freedom of belief, even if our words or beliefs denigrate the humanity of others. Yet, while we are each free to believe whatever we choose, we cannot do whatever we choose, not in a world where we protect the human rights of all.

Reaching understanding of these issues takes more than speech. It does take a conversation. In fact, it takes a constellation of conversations in places big and small. And it takes a willingness to see stark differences in belief as a reason to begin the conversation, not to avoid it.

But progress comes from changes in laws. In many places, including my own country, legal protections have preceded, not followed, broader recognition of rights. Laws have a teaching effect. Laws that discriminate validate other kinds of discrimination. Laws that require equal protections reinforce the moral imperative of equality. And practically speaking, it is often the case that laws must change before fears about change dissipate.

Many in my country thought that President Truman was making a grave error when he ordered the racial desegregation of our military. They argued that it would undermine unit cohesion. And it wasn't until he went ahead and did it that we saw how it strengthened our social fabric in ways even the supporters of the policy could not foresee. Likewise, some worried in my country that the repeal of "Don't Ask, Don't Tell" would have a negative effect on our armed forces. Now, the Marine Corps Commandant, who was one of the strongest voices against the repeal, says that his concerns were unfounded and that the Marines have embraced the change.

Finally, progress comes from being willing to walk a mile in someone else's shoes. We need to ask ourselves, "How would it feel if it were a crime to love the person I love? How would it feel to be discriminated against for something about myself that I cannot change?" This challenge applies to all of us as we reflect upon deeply held beliefs, as we work to embrace tolerance and respect for the dignity of all persons, and as we engage humbly with those with whom we disagree in the hope of creating greater understanding.

A fifth and final question is how we do our part to bring the world to embrace human rights for all people including LGBT people. Yes, LGBT people must help lead this effort, as so many of you are. Their knowledge and experiences are invaluable and their courage inspirational. We know the names of brave LGBT activists who have literally given their lives for this cause, and there are many more whose names we will never know. But often those who are denied rights are least empowered to bring about the changes they seek. Acting alone, minorities can never achieve the majorities necessary for political change.

So, when any part of humanity is sidelined, the rest of us cannot sit on the sidelines. Every time a barrier to progress has fallen, it has taken a cooperative effort from those on both sides of the barrier. In the fight for women's rights, the support of men remains crucial. The fight for racial equality has relied on contributions from people of all races. Combating Islamophobia or antisemitism is a task for people of all faiths. And the same is true with this struggle for equality.

Conversely, when we see denials and abuses of human rights and fail to act, that sends the message to those deniers and abusers that they won't suffer any consequences for their actions, and so they carry on. But when we do act, we send a powerful moral message. Right here in Geneva, the international community acted this year to strengthen a global consensus around the human rights of LGBT people. At the Human Rights Council in March, eighty-five countries from all regions supported a statement calling for an end to criminalization and violence against people because of their sexual orientation and gender identity.

At the following session of the Council in June, South Africa took the lead on a resolution about violence against LGBT people. The delegation from South Africa spoke eloquently about their own experience and struggle for human equality and its indivisibility. When the measure passed, it became the first-ever U.N. resolution recognizing the human rights of gay people worldwide. In the Organization of American States this year, the Inter-American Commission on Human Rights created a unit on the rights of LGBT people, a step toward what we hope will be the creation of a special rapporteur.

Now, we must go further and work here and in every region of the world to galvanize more support for the human rights of the LGBT community. To the leaders of those countries where people are jailed, beaten, or executed for being gay, I ask you to consider this: Leadership, by definition, means being out in front of your people when it is called for. It means standing up for the dignity of all your citizens and persuading your people to do the same. It also means ensuring that all citizens are treated as equals under your laws, because let me be clear—I am not saying that gay people can't or don't commit crimes. They can and they do, just like straight people. And when they do, they should be held accountable, but it should never be a crime to be gay.

And to people of all nations, I say supporting human rights is your responsibility too. The lives of gay people are shaped not only by laws, but by the treatment they receive every day from their families, from their neighbors. Eleanor Roosevelt, who did so much to advance human rights worldwide, said that these rights begin in the small places close to home—the streets where people live, the schools they attend, the factories, farms, and offices where they work. These places are your domain. The actions you take, the ideals that you advocate, can determine whether human rights flourish where you are.

And finally, to LGBT men and women worldwide, let me say this: Wherever you live and whatever the circumstances of your life, whether you are connected to a network of support or feel isolated and vulnerable, please know that you are not alone. People around the globe are working hard to support you and to bring an end to the injustices and dangers you face. That is certainly true for my country. And you have an ally in the United States of America, and you have millions of friends among the American people.

The Obama administration defends the human rights of LGBT people as part of our comprehensive human rights policy and as a priority of our foreign policy. In our embassies, our diplomats are raising concerns about specific cases and laws, and working with a range of partners to strengthen human rights protections for all. In Washington, we have created a task force at the State Department to support and coordinate this work. And in the coming months, we will provide every embassy with a toolkit to help improve their efforts. And we have created a program that offers emergency support to defenders of human rights for LGBT people.

This morning, back in Washington, President Obama put into place the first U.S. government strategy dedicated to combating human rights abuses against LGBT persons abroad. Building on efforts already underway at the State Department and across the government, the president has directed all U.S. government agencies engaged overseas to combat the criminalization of LGBT status and conduct, to enhance efforts to protect vulnerable LGBT refugees and asylum seekers, to ensure that our foreign assistance promotes the protection of LGBT rights, to enlist international organizations in the fight against discrimination, and to respond swiftly to abuses against LGBT persons.

I am also pleased to announce that we are launching a new Global Equality Fund that will support the work of civil society organizations working on these issues around the world. This fund will help them record facts so they can target their advocacy, learn how to use the law as a tool, manage their budgets, train their staffs, and forge partnerships with women's organizations and other human rights groups. We have committed more than $3 million to start this fund, and we have hope that others will join us in supporting it.

The women and men who advocate for human rights for the LGBT community in hostile places, some of whom are here today with us, are brave and dedicated, and deserve all the help we can give them. We know the road ahead will not be easy. A great deal of work lies before us. But many of us have seen firsthand how quickly change can come. In our lifetimes, attitudes toward gay people in many places have been transformed. Many people, including myself, have experienced a deepening of our own convictions on this topic over the years, as we have devoted more thought to it, engaged in dialogues and debates, and established personal and professional relationships with people who are gay.

This evolution is evident in many places. To highlight one example, the Delhi High Court decriminalized homosexuality in India two years ago, writing, and I quote, "If there is one tenet that can be said to be an underlying theme of the Indian constitution, it is inclusiveness." There is little doubt in my mind that support for LGBT human rights will continue to climb. Because for many young people, this is simple: all people deserve to be treated with dignity and have their human rights respected, no matter who they are or whom they love.

There is a phrase that people in the United States invoke when urging others to support human rights: "Be on the right side of history." The story of the United States is the story of a nation that has repeatedly grappled with intolerance and inequality. We fought a brutal civil war over slavery. People from coast to coast joined in campaigns to recognize the rights of women, indigenous peoples, racial minorities, children, people with disabilities, immigrants, workers, and on and on. And the march toward equality and justice has continued. Those who advocate for expanding the circle of human rights were and are on the right side of history, and history honors them. Those who tried to constrict human rights were wrong, and history reflects that as well.

I know that the thoughts I've shared today involve questions on which opinions are still evolving. As it has happened so many times before, opinion will converge once again with the truth, the immutable truth, that all persons are created free and equal in dignity and rights. We are called once more to make real the words of the Universal Declaration. Let us answer that call. Let us be on the right side of history, for our people, our nations, and future generations, whose lives will be shaped by the work we do today. I come before you with great hope and confidence that no matter how long the road ahead, we will travel it successfully together.

Thank you very much.

CHAPTER 11

Elizabeth Warren

The Path to Equality

2015

The first civil rights battles were hard fought. But they estab-lished that Black Lives Matter. That Black Citizens Matter. That Black Families Matter. Half a century later, we have made real progress, but we have not made ENOUGH progress.

E lizabeth Warren, senator for Massachusetts, is often con-sidered one of the more liberal members of the Democratic caucus and has made championing equality a signature issue throughout her career. In this address, she reminds us that racial equality is a fundamental American right. She frames the speech with a historical narrative of what America looked like at the onset of the Civil Rights Movement of the 1960s, juxtaposing areas where progress has been made against areas that have changed shock-ingly little. She references the legacies of President John F. Kennedy, Senator Edward Kennedy, and Martin Luther King Jr. to ask if we have delivered on the ideas they championed. Key lines in this speech drive home the theme that Black Lives Matter.

In the spring of 2020, the murder of George Floyd prompted public figures on both sides of the aisle to deliver speeches calling for America to hold itself to its highest ideals, leading to a reawakening of conversations related to diversity, equity, and inclusion. The matter has since become highly charged; while people generally agree that equality for all is a shared value, the political right and left sharply disagree about whether private- and public-sector remedies are necessary. Interestingly, to today's reader, Warren's speech was not delivered in the wake of George Floyd's murder in 2020—when Black Lives Matter became a defining topic in the national conversation—but five years earlier, in 2015.

While Warren is at times antagonistic in her views towards Republicans, the remarkable thing about this speech is the timelessness of its themes on justice and civil rights. Whether in 2015, 2020, today, or any time after the 1960s, Warren reminds America that we need to confront inequities with a lens that offers equal opportunity and protections in law, commerce, and society. While each reader of this book may have different views on the specifics of the policy proposals outlined in her speech, Warren's ability to connect the past to the present to acknowledge both sides of the debate and her call that as a nation we must live to our highest ideals are notions that everyone can agree on.

Thank you. I'm grateful to be here at the Edward M. Kennedy Institute for the United States Senate. This place is a fitting tribute to our champion, Ted Kennedy. A man of courage, compassion, and commitment, who taught us what public service is all about. Not a day goes by that we don't miss his passion, his enthusiasm, and—most of all— his dedication to all of our working families.

As the Senior Senator from Massachusetts, I have the great honor of sitting at Senator Kennedy's desk—right over there. The original, back in Washington, is a little more dented and scratched, but it has something very special in the drawer. Ted Kennedy carved his name in it. When I sit at my desk, sometimes when I'm waiting to speak or to vote, I open the drawer and run my thumb across his name. It reminds me of the high expectations of the people of Massachusetts, and I try, every day, to live up to the legacy he left behind.

Senator Kennedy took office just over fifty years ago, in the midst of one of the great moral and political debates in American history—the debate over the Civil Rights Act. In his first speech on the floor of the Senate, just four months after his brother's assassination, he stood up to support equal rights for all Americans. He ended that speech with a powerful personal message about what the civil rights struggle meant to the late President Kennedy:

> *His heart and soul are in this bill. If his life and death had a meaning, it was that we should not hate but love one another; we should use our powers not to create conditions of oppression that lead to violence, but conditions of freedom that lead to peace.*

That's what I'd like to talk about today.

A half-century ago, when Senator Kennedy spoke of the Civil Rights Act, entrenched, racist power did everything it could to sustain oppression of African Americans, and violence was its first tool. Lynchings, terrorism, intimidation. The 16th Street Baptist Church. Medgar Evers. Emmett Till. When Alabama Governor George Wallace stood before the nation and declared during his 1963 inaugural address that he would defend 'segregation now, segregation tomorrow, segregation forever,' he made clear that the state would stand with those who used violence.

But violence was not the only tool. African Americans were effectively stripped of citizenship when they were denied the right to vote. The tools varied—literacy tests, poll taxes, moral character tests, grandfather clauses—but the results were the same. They were denied basic rights of citizenship and the chance to participate in self-government.

The third tool of oppression was to deliberately deny millions of African Americans economic opportunities solely because of the color of their skin.

I have often spoken about how America built a great middle class. Coming out of the Great Depression, from the 1930s to the late 1970s, as GDP went up, wages went up for most Americans. But there's a dark underbelly to that story. While median family income in America was growing—for both white and African American families—African American incomes were only a fraction of white incomes. In the mid-1950s, the median income for African American families was just a little more than half the income of white families.

And the problem went beyond just income. Look at housing: for most middle-class families in America, buying a home is the number one way to build wealth. It's a retirement plan—pay off the house and live on Social Security. An investment option—mortgage the house to start a business. It's a way to help the kids get through college, a safety net if someone gets really sick, and, if all goes well and Grandma and Grandpa can hang on to the house until they die, it's a way to give the next generation a boost—extra money to move the family up the ladder.

For much of the twentieth century, that's how it worked for generation after generation of white Americans—but not black Americans. Entire legal structures were created to prevent African Americans from building economic security through homeownership. Legally enforced segregation. Restrictive deeds. Redlining. Land contracts. Coming out of the Great Depression, America built a middle class, but systematic discrimination kept most African American families from being part of it.

State-sanctioned discrimination wasn't limited to homeownership. The government enforced discrimination in public accommodations, discrimination in schools, discrimination in credit—it was a long and spiteful list.

Economic justice is not—and has never been—sufficient to ensure racial justice. Owning a home won't stop someone from burning a cross on the front lawn. Admission to a school won't prevent a beating on the sidewalk outside. But when Dr. King led hundreds of thousands of people to march on Washington, he talked about an end to violence, access to voting, *and* economic opportunity. As Dr. King once wrote, "the inseparable twin of racial injustice was economic injustice."

The tools of oppression were woven together, and the civil rights struggle was fought against that oppression wherever it was found—against violence, against the denial of voting rights, and against economic injustice.

The battles were bitter and sometimes deadly. Firehoses turned on peaceful protestors. Police officers setting their dogs to attack black students. Bloody Sunday at the Edmund Pettus Bridge.

But the Civil Rights Movement pushed this country in a new direction.

The federal government cracked down on state-sponsored violence. Presidents Eisenhower, Kennedy, and Johnson all called out the National Guard, and, in doing so, declared that everyone had a right to equal protection under the law, guaranteed by the Constitution. Congress protected the rights of all citizens to vote with the Voting Rights Act.

And economic opportunities opened up when Congress passed civil rights laws that protected equal access to employment, public accommodations, and housing.

In the same way that the tools of oppression were woven together, a package of civil rights laws came together to protect black people from violence, to ensure access to the ballot box, and to build economic opportunity. Or to say it another way, these laws made three powerful declarations: Black lives matter. Black citizens matter. Black families matter.

Fifty years later, we have made real progress toward creating the conditions of freedom—but we have not made *enough* progress.

Fifty years later, violence against African Americans has not disappeared. Consider law enforcement. The vast majority of police officers sign up so they can protect their communities. They are part of an honorable profession that takes risks every day to keep us safe. We know that. But we also know—and say—the names of those whose lives have been treated with callous indifference. Sandra Bland. Freddie Gray. Michael Brown. We've seen sickening videos of unarmed, black Americans cut down by bullets, choked to death while gasping for air—their lives ended by those who are sworn to protect them. Peaceful, unarmed protestors have been beaten. Journalists have been jailed. And, in some cities, white vigilantes with weapons freely walk the streets. And it's not just about law enforcement either. Just look to the terrorism this summer at Emanuel AME Church. We must be honest: Fifty years after John Kennedy and Martin Luther King, Jr. spoke out, violence against African Americans has not disappeared.

And what about voting rights? Two years ago, five conservative justices on the Supreme Court gutted the Voting Rights Act, opening the floodgates ever wider for measures designed to suppress minority voting. Today, the specific tools of oppression have changed—voter ID laws, racial gerrymandering, and mass disfranchisement through a criminal justice system that disproportionately incarcerates black citizens. The tools have changed, but black voters are still deliberately cut out of the political process.

Violence. Voting. And what about economic injustice? Research shows that the legal changes in the civil rights era created new employment and housing opportunities. In the 1960s and the 1970s, African American men and women began to close the wage gap with white workers, giving millions of black families hope that they might build real wealth.

But then, Republicans' trickle-down economic theory arrived. Just as this country was taking the first steps toward economic justice, the Republicans pushed a theory that meant helping the richest people and the most powerful corporations get richer and more powerful. I'll just do one statistic on this: From 1980 to 2012, GDP continued to rise, but how much of the income growth went to the 90 percent of America—everyone outside the top 10 percent—black, white, Latino? None. Zero. Nothing. 100 percent of all the new income produced in this country over the past thirty years has gone to the top 10 percent.

Today, 90 percent of Americans see no real wage growth. For African Americans, who were so far behind earlier in the twentieth century, this means that since the 1980s they have been hit particularly hard. In January of this year, African American unemployment was 10.3 percent—more than twice the rate of white unemployment. And, after beginning to make progress during the civil rights era to close the wealth gap between black and white families, in the 1980s the wealth gap exploded, so that from 1984 to 2009, the wealth gap between black and white families tripled.

The 2008 housing collapse destroyed trillions in family wealth across the country, but the crash hit African Americans like a punch in the gut. Because middle-class black families' wealth was disproportionately tied up in homeownership and not other forms of savings, these families were hit harder by the housing collapse. But they also got hit harder because of discriminatory lending practices—yes, discriminatory lending practices in the twenty-first century. Recently, several big banks and other mortgage lenders paid hundreds of millions in fines, admitting that they illegally steered black and Latino borrowers into more expensive mortgages than white borrowers who had similar credit. Tom Perez, who at the time was the assistant attorney general for civil rights, called it a "racial surtax." And it's still happening—earlier this month, the National Fair Housing Alliance filed a discrimination complaint against real estate agents in Mississippi after an investigation showed those agents consistently steering white buyers away from interracial neighborhoods and black buyers away from affluent ones. Another investigation showed similar results across our nation's cities. Housing discrimination [is] alive and well in 2015.

Violence, voting, economic justice.

We have made important strides forward. But we are not done yet. And now, it is our time.

I speak today with the full knowledge that I have not personally experienced and can never truly understand the fear, the oppression, and the pain that confronts African Americans every day. But none of us can ignore what is happening in this country. Not when our black friends, family, neighbors literally fear dying in the streets.

Listen to the brave, powerful voices of today's new generation of civil rights leaders. Incredible voices. Listen to them say: "If I die in police custody, know that I did not commit suicide." Watch them march through the streets, "hands up, don't shoot"—not to incite a riot, but to fight for their lives. To fight for their lives.

This is the reality all of us must confront, as uncomfortable and ugly as that reality may be. It comes to us to once again affirm that black lives matter, that black citizens matter, that black families matter.

Once again, the task begins with safeguarding our communities from violence. We have made progress, but it is a tragedy when any American cannot trust those who have sworn to protect and serve. This pervasive and persistent distrust isn't based on myths. It is grounded in the reality of unjustified violence.

Policing must become a truly community endeavor—not in just a few cities, but everywhere. Police forces should look like, and come from, the neighborhoods they serve. They should reach out to support and defend the community—working with people in neighborhoods before problems arise. All police forces—not just some—must be trained to de-escalate and to avoid the likelihood of violence. Body cameras can help us know what happens when someone is hurt.

We honor the bravery and sacrifice that our law enforcement officers show every day on the job—and the noble intentions of the vast majority of those who take up the difficult job of keeping us safe. But police are not occupying armies. This is America, not a war zone—and policing practices in all cities, not just some, need to reflect that.

Next, voting.

It's time to call out the recent flurry of new state law restrictions for what they are: An all-out campaign by Republicans to take away the right to vote from poor and black and Latino American citizens who probably won't vote for them. The push to restrict voting is nothing more than a naked grab to win elections that they can't win if every citizen votes.

Two years ago, the Supreme Court eviscerated critical parts of the Voting Rights Act. Congress could easily fix this, and Democrats in the Senate have called for restoration of voting rights. Now it is time for Republicans to step up to support a restoration of the Voting Rights Act—or to stand before the American people and explain why they have abandoned America's most cherished liberty, the right to vote.

And while we're at it, we need to update the rules around voting. Voting should be simple. Voter registration should be automatic. Get a driver's license, get registered automatically. Nonviolent, law-abiding citizens should not lose the right to vote because of a prior conviction. Election Day should be a holiday, so no one has to choose between a paycheck and a vote. Early voting and vote by mail would give fast food and retail workers who don't get holiday days off a chance to proudly cast their votes. The hidden discrimination that comes with purging voter rolls and short-staffing polling places must stop. The right to vote remains essential to protect all other rights, and no candidate for president or for any other elected office—Republican or Democrat—should be elected if they will not pledge to support full, meaningful voting rights.

Finally, economic justice. Our task will not be complete until we ensure that every family—regardless of race—has a fighting chance to build an economic future for themselves and their families. We need less talk and more action about reducing unemployment, ending wage stagnation, and closing the income gap between white and nonwhite workers.

And one more issue, dear to my heart: It's time to come down hard on predatory practices that allow financial institutions to systematically strip wealth out of communities of color. One of the ugly consequences of bank deregulation was that there was no cop on the beat when too many financial institutions figured out that they could make great money by tricking, trapping, and defrauding targeted families. Now we have a Consumer Financial Protection Bureau, and we need to make sure it stays strong and independent so that it can do its job and make credit markets work for black families, Latino families, white families—all families.

Yes, there's work to do.

Back in March, I met an elderly man at the First Baptist Church in Montgomery, Alabama. We were having coffee and donuts in the church basement before the service started. He told me that more than fifty years earlier—in May of 1961—he had spent eleven hours in that same basement, along with hundreds of people, while a mob outside threatened to burn down the church because it was a sanctuary for civil rights workers. Dr. King called

attorney general Bobby Kennedy, desperately asking for
help. The attorney general promised to send the Army, but
the closest military base was several hours away. So the
members of the church and the civil rights workers waited
in the sweltering basement, crowded together, listening to
the mob outside and hoping the U.S. Army would arrive
in time.

After the church service, I asked Congressman John
Lewis about that night. He had been right there in that
church back in 1961 while the mob gathered outside. He
had been in the room during the calls to the attorney general. I asked if he had been afraid that the Army wouldn't
make it in time. He said that he was "never, ever afraid.
You come to that point where you lose all sense of fear."
And then he said something I'll never forget. He said that
his parents didn't want him to get involved in civil rights.
They didn't want him to "cause trouble." But he had done
it anyway. He told me: "Sometimes it is important to cause
necessary trouble."

The first civil rights battles were hard fought. But they
established that Black Lives Matter. That Black Citizens
Matter. That Black Families Matter. Half a century
later, we have made real progress, but we have not made
enough progress. As Senator Kennedy said in his first-floor
speech, "This is not a political issue. It is a moral issue,
to be resolved through political means." So it comes to
us to continue the fight, to make, as John Lewis said, the
"necessary trouble" until we can truly say that in America,
every citizen enjoys the conditions of freedom.

Thank you.

CHAPTER 12

Barack Obama

The Affordable Care Act

2016

Because of Obamacare, another twenty million Americans now know the financial security of health insurance. So do another three million children, thanks in large part to the Affordable Care Act and the improvements, the enhancements that we made to the Children's Health Insurance Program. And the net result is that never in American history has the uninsured rate been lower than it is today.

The Affordable Care Act will likely be remembered as one of the signature achievements of Barack Obama's presidency. The 2010 law expanded access to health care to twenty-five million uninsured individuals and was the first successful major reform to the corporate-payer model since Medicare and Medicaid were established over fifty years before. Obamacare—as it is frequently called—was controversial at the time it was passed.

Supporters argued that it was hard for those without employer-sponsored health insurance to access affordable plans. Opponents said it was too costly, and that it impeded on people's personal right to self-determination—the right to not have health insurance—and that the private sector was better suited to come up with solutions than the federal government. History ultimately proved the naysayers wrong. From 2010 to 2015, the uninsured rate declined from 16 percent to 9.1 percent, or 20 million individuals, with an additional 20 million individuals believed to be covered who would not have been without the law.

This speech was given by Obama in 2016, near the end of his second term in office and six years after the Affordable Care Act was passed. Obama used the speech to talk about his signature piece of legislation, giving real-world examples of individuals who it had helped. The controversy over Obamacare had largely faded at this point in the president's second term. The legislation proved to be more successful than people thought. It enrolled millions on insurance plans, did not bankrupt the country, and was becoming viewed as providing a net positive. By early 2017, the majority of Americans had a favorable opinion of the law.

Obama took some rare rhetorical moves in this speech. He showed unusual humility as a sitting president, acknowledging that the ACA was not perfect and needed to be reformed. He also cited the concerns of the average American by calling out real people who the ACA benefited. This struck a delicate balance between promoting his accomplishments and humanizing the speech with heartwarming stories while at the same time noting the law could do better, citing areas where the ACA didn't live up to its potential. Some of these weaknesses were due to the political compromises made six years earlier to get the ACA passed, and some were because in any incredibly complex government-backed program, there are inevitable tweaks to be made.

History is often the best judge of policy. What proved to be one of the most controversial issues of the 2008 presidential campaign—whether there should be a nationally-supported health insurance program—is taken as a given by most people today. The ACA proved to be extremely popular and is an example of how a once-partisan issue, in this case originally championed by Democrats, can become a mainstream centrist policy that is accepted as the norm over time. While Republicans and Democrats may differ on specific aspects of policy regarding benefits and coverage, or how state marketplaces should work, the fact that all should have some form of access to health care is a matter almost everyone can agree on.

The first thing I want to say is thank you for your support and thank you for the opportunity and the privilege you've given me to serve these past eight years. I remember standing just a few blocks north of here in the closing days of the 2008 campaign. And at that point, we were already realizing that we were in the midst of the worst economic crisis of our lifetimes. We didn't know where the bottom would be. We were still in the middle of two wars. Over 150,000 of our troops were overseas. But thanks to the hard work and the determination of the American people, when I come here today, the story is different.

Working together, we've cut the unemployment rate in Florida by more than half. Across the country, we turned years of job losses into the longest streak of job creation on record. We slashed our dependence on foreign oil, doubled our production of renewable energy. Incomes are rising again—they rose more last year than any time ever recorded. Poverty is falling—[it] fell more last year than any time since 1968. Our graduation rates from high school are at record highs. College enrollment is significantly higher than it was when we came into office. Marriage equality is a reality in all fifty states.

So, we've been busy. This is why I've got gray hair. But we did one other thing. We fought to make sure that in America, health care is not just a privilege, but a right for every single American. And that's what I want to talk about today.

You've heard a lot about Obamacare, as it's come to be known. You heard a lot about it in the six and a half years since I signed it into law. And some of the things you heard might even be true. But one thing I want to start with is just reminding people why it is that we fought for health reform in the first place. Because it was one of the key motivators in my campaign.

And it wasn't just because rising health costs were eating into workers' paychecks and straining budgets for businesses and for governments. It wasn't just because, before the law was passed, insurance companies could just drop your coverage because you got sick, right at the time you needed insurance most.

It was because of you. It was because of the stories that I was hearing all around the country, and right here in Florida—hearing from people who had been forced to fight a broken health care system at the same time as they were fighting to get well.

It was about children like Zoe Lihn, who needed heart surgery when she was just fifteen hours old—just a baby, just [an] infant. And she was halfway to hitting her lifetime insurance cap before she was old enough to walk. Her parents had no idea how they could possibly make sure that she continued to make progress. And today, because of the Affordable Care Act, Zoe is in first grade and she's loving martial arts. And she's got a bright future ahead of her.

We fought so hard for health reform because of women like Amanda Heidel, who lives here in South Florida. As a girl, she was diagnosed with diabetes—and that's a disease with costs that can add up quickly if you don't have insurance. [It] can eat away at your dreams. But thanks to the Affordable Care Act, Amanda got to stay on her parents' plan after college. When she turned twenty-six, Amanda went online; she shopped for an affordable health insurance plan that covered her medications. Today, she's pursuing a doctorate in psychology. And Amanda said that the Affordable Care Act "has given me the security and freedom to choose how I live my life." *The freedom and security to choose how I live my life.* That's what this was all about.

Zoe and Amanda, the people who I get letters from every single day describing what it meant not to fear that if they got sick, or a member of their family got sick; if they, heaven forbid, were in an accident, that somehow they could lose everything.

So, because of this law, because of Obamacare, another twenty million Americans now know the financial security of health insurance. So do another three million children, thanks in large part to the Affordable Care Act and the improvements, the enhancements that we made to the Children's Health Insurance Program. And the net result is that never in American history has the uninsured rate been lower than it is today. Never. And that's true across the board. It's dropped among women. It's dropped among Latinos and African Americans, every other demographic group. It's worked.

Now, that doesn't mean that it's perfect. No law is. And it's true that a lot of the noise around the health care debate, ever since we tried to pass this law, has been nothing more than politics. But we've also always known, and I have always said, that for all the good that the Affordable Care Act is doing right now—for as big a step forward as it was—it's still just a first step. It's like building a starter home, or buying a starter home. It's a lot better than not having a home, but you hope that over time you make some improvements.

And, in fact, since we first signed the law, we've already taken a number of steps to improve it. And we can do even more—but only if we put aside all the political rhetoric, all the partisanship, and just be honest about what's working, what needs fixing, and how we fix it.

So that's what I want to do today. This isn't kind of a rah-rah speech. I might get into the details. I hope you don't mind.

So, let's start with a basic fact. The majority of Americans do not—let me repeat—do not get health care through the Affordable Care Act. Eighty percent or so of Americans get health care on the job, through their employer, or they get health care through Medicaid, or they get health care through Medicare. And so, for most Americans, the Affordable Care Act, Obama, has not affected your coverage—except to make it stronger.

Because of the law, you now have free preventive care. Insurance companies have to offer that in whatever policy they sell. Because of the law, you now have free checkups for women. Because of the law, you get free mammograms. Because of the law, it is harder for insurance companies to discriminate against you because you're a woman when you get health insurance. Because of the law, doctors are finding better ways to perform heart surgeries and delivering healthier babies, and treating chronic disease, and reducing the number of people that, once they're in the hospital, end up having to return to the hospital.

So, you're getting better quality even though you don't know that Obamacare is doing it.

Because of the law, your annual out-of-pocket spending is capped. Seniors get discounts on their prescription drugs because of the law. Young people can stay on their parents' plan—just like Amanda did—because of the law. And Amanda was able to stay on her parents' plan and then get insurance after she aged out, even though she has what used to be called a preexisting condition—because we made it illegal to discriminate against people with preexisting conditions.

By the way, before this law, before Obamacare, health insurance rates for everybody—whether you got your insurance on the job, or you were buying it on your own— health insurance rates generally were going up really fast. This law has actually slowed down the pace of health care inflation. So, every year premiums have gone up, but they've gone up the slowest in fifty years since Obamacare was passed. In fact, if your family gets insurance through your job, your family is paying, on average, about $3,600 less per year than you would be if the cost trends that had existed before the law were passed had continued. Think about that. That's money in your pocket.

Now, some people may say, well, I've seen my co-pays go up, or my networks have changed. But these are decisions that are made by your employers. It's not because of Obamacare. They're not determined by the Affordable Care Act.

So, if the Affordable Care Act, if Obamacare hasn't changed the coverage of the 80 percent of Americans who already had insurance, except to make it a better value, except to make it more reliable, how has the law impacted the other 15 or 20 percent of Americans who didn't have health insurance through their job, or didn't qualify for Medicaid, or didn't qualify for Medicare?

Well, before the Affordable Care Act, frankly, you were probably out of luck. Either you had to buy health insurance on your own, because you weren't getting it through the job, and it was wildly expensive, and your premiums were going up all the time, and if you happened to get sick and use the insurance, the insurer the next year could drop you. And if you had had an illness like cancer or diabetes, or some other chronic disease, you couldn't buy new insurance because the insurance company's attitude was, you know what, this is just going to cost us money; we don't want to insure you.

So, if you were trying to buy health insurance on your own, it was either hugely expensive or didn't provide very effective coverage. You might buy a policy thinking that it was going to cover you. It was sort of like when I was young and I bought my first car, I had to buy car insurance. And I won't name the insurance company, but I bought the insurance because it was the law, and I got the cheapest one I could get, because I didn't have any money—and it was a really beat-up car. And I remember somebody rear-ends me, and I call up the insurance company, thinking maybe I can get some help, and they laughed at me. They're all like, what, are you kidding? It didn't provide any coverage other than essentially allowing me to drive.

Well, that's what it was like for a lot of people who didn't have health insurance on the job. So that meant that a lot of people just didn't bother getting health insurance at all. And when they got sick, they'd have to go to the emergency room.

And so you're relying on the emergency room, but the emergency room is the most expensive place to get care.

And because you weren't insured, the hospital would have to give you the care for free, and they would have to then make up for those costs by charging everybody else more money. So, it wasn't good for anybody.

So, what the Affordable Care Act is designed to do is to help those people who were previously either uninsured or underinsured. And it worked to help those people in two ways.

First, we gave states funding to expand Medicaid to cover more people. In D.C. and the thirty-one states that took us up on that, more than four million people have coverage who didn't have it before. They now have health insurance.

Second, for people who made too much to qualify for Medicaid even after we expanded it, we set up what we call marketplaces on HealthCare.gov, so you could shop for a plan that fits your needs, and then we would give you tax credits to help you buy it. And most people today can find a plan for less than $75 a month at the HealthCare .gov marketplace when you include the tax credits that government is giving you. That means it's less than your cellphone bill—because I know you guys are tweeting a lot and texting and selfies. And the good news is, is that most people who end up buying their coverage through the marketplaces, using these tax credits, are satisfied with their plans.

So not only did Obamacare do a lot of good for the 80-plus percent of Americans who already had health care, but now it gave a new affordable option to a lot of folks who never had options before. All told, about another 10 percent of the country now have coverage.

The Affordable Care Act has done what it was designed to do: It gave us affordable health care.

So what's the problem? Why is there still such a fuss? Well, part of the problem is the fact that a Democratic president named Barack Obama passed the law. And that's just the truth. I mean, I worked really, really hard to engage Republicans; took Republican ideas that originally they had praised; said, let's work together to get this done. And when they just refused to do anything, we said, all right, we're going to have to do it with Democrats. And that's what we did.

And early on, Republicans just decided to oppose it. And then they tried to scare people with all kinds of predictions—that it would be a job-killer; that it would force everyone into government-run insurance; that it would lead to rationing; that it would lead to death panels; that it would bankrupt the federal government. You remember all this. And despite the fact that all the bad things they predicted have not actually happened, despite the fact that we've created more jobs since the bill passed in consecutive months than any time on record, despite the fact that the uninsured rate has gone down to its lowest levels ever, despite that fact that it's actually cost less than anybody anticipated and has shown to be much less disruptive on existing plans that people get through their employers, despite the fact that it saved Medicare over $150 billion—which makes that program more secure—despite all this, it's been hard, if not impossible, for any Republican to admit it.

They just can't admit that a lot of good things have happened and the bad things they predicted didn't happen. So they just keep on repeating, we're going to repeal it. We're going to repeal it, and we're going to replace it with something better—even though, six and a half years later, they haven't—they still haven't shown us what it is that they would do that would be better.

But—and this is actually the main reason I'm here—just because a lot of the Republican criticism has proven to be false and politically motivated doesn't mean that there aren't some legitimate concerns about how the law is working now. And the main issue has to do with the folks who still aren't getting enough help. Remember, I said 80 percent of people, even before the law passed, already had health insurance. And then we expanded Medicaid, and we set up the marketplaces, and another 10 percent of people got health insurance. Well, but that still leaves that last 10 percent. And the fact that that last 10 percent still has difficulties is something that we've got to do something about.

Now, part of the reason for this is, as I already mentioned to you, not every state expanded Medicaid to its citizens, which means that some of the most vulnerable working families that the law was designed to help still haven't gotten insurance. As you may have heard, Florida is one of those states. If your governor could put politics aside—

AUDIENCE: Booo—

THE PRESIDENT: Don't boo—vote.

If your governor would just put politics aside and do what's right, then more than 700,000 Floridians would suddenly have access to coverage. And, by the way, that would hold down costs for the rest of you, because there would be less uncompensated care in hospitals. And it means that people who did sign up for the marketplace, who oftentimes may be sicker, qualify for Medicaid, and so they're not raising costs in the marketplace.

In fact, if the nineteen states who so far have not expanded Medicaid would just do so, another four million people would have coverage right now all across the country.

So that's step number one. And that's, by the way, just completely in the control of these governors. They could be doing it—right now. They could do it tomorrow.

Now, the second issue has to do with the marketplaces. Although the marketplaces are working well in most of the states, there are some states where there's still not enough competition between insurers. So if you only have one insurer, they may decide we're going to jack up rates because we can, because nobody else is offering a better price.

In those states where the governor or legislature is hostile to the ACA, it makes it harder to enroll people because the state is not actively participating in outreach. And so, as a consequence, in those states enrollment in the plan—especially enrollment of young people—has lagged.

And what that means is that the insurance pool is smaller and it gets a higher percentage of older and sicker people who are signing up—because if you're sick or you're old, you're more likely to say, well, I'm going to sign up, no matter what, because I know I'm going to need it; if you're young and healthy like you guys, you say, eh, I'm fine, life is good—so you have more older and sicker people signing up, fewer younger and healthier people signing up, and that drives rates up, because the people who use health care most end up being in the insurance pool; people who use it least are not.

And then, in some cases, insurers just set their prices too low at the outset because they didn't know what the insurance pool was going to look like, and then they started losing money. And so now they've decided to significantly increase premiums in some states.

Now, it's these premium increases in some of the states in the marketplace that sometimes attracts negative headlines. Remember, these premium increases won't impact most of the people who are buying insurance through the marketplace, because even when premiums go up, the tax credits go up to offset the increases. So people who qualify for tax credits—they may not even notice their premiums went up because the tax credit is covered.

And keep in mind that these premium increases that some of you may have read about have no effect at all if you're getting health insurance on the job, or through Medicaid or Medicare. So, for the 80 [percent]-plus people who already had health insurance, if your premium is going up, it's not because of Obamacare. It's because of your employer or your insurer—even though sometimes they try to blame Obamacare for why the rates go up. It's not because of any policy of the Affordable Care Act that the rates are going up.

But if you are one of the people who doesn't get health care on the job, doesn't qualify for Medicaid, doesn't qualify for Medicare, doesn't qualify for a tax credit to help you buy insurance, because maybe you made just a little bit too much money under the law—these premium increases do make insurance less affordable. And in some states, the premium increases are manageable. Some are 2 percent or 8 percent; some 20 percent. But we know there are some states that may see premiums go up by 50 percent or more.

And an extreme example is Arizona, where we expect benchmark premiums will more than double. Part of this is because Arizona is one of those states that had really low average premiums—among the lowest in the country—so now insurance companies basically are trying to catch up, and they also don't have a lot of competition there. And meanwhile, in states like Florida, the failure to expand Medicaid contributes to higher marketplace premiums. And then there are some other states that just because of the nature of their health care systems, or the fact that they're rural and people are dispersed, so it's harder to provide health care, more expensive—they have a tougher time controlling costs generally.

Again, the tax credits in the ACA will protect most consumers from the brunt of these premium increases. And with the ability to shop around on HealthCare.gov—which works really well now—most people can find plans for prices even lower than this year's prices. But there are going to be people who are hurt by premium increases or a lack of competition and choice. And I don't want to see anybody left out without health insurance. I don't want to see any family having to choose between health insurance now or saving for retirement, or saving for their kids' college education, or just paying their own bills.

So the question we should be asking is, what do we do about these growing pains in the Affordable Care Act, and how do we get the last 9 percent of Americans covered? How do we reach those last 9 percent? And how do we make sure that premiums are more stable going forward, and the marketplace insurance pools are more stable going forward?

Well, I can tell you what will not work. Repealing the Affordable Care Act will not work. That's a bad idea. That will not solve the problem. Because right off the bat, repeal would take away health care from twenty million people. We'd go back where 80 percent of people had health insurance instead of 90 percent, right off the bat.

And all the reforms that everybody benefits from that I talked about—like young Americans being able to stay on their parents' plans, or the rules that prevent insurance companies from discriminating against people because of a preexisting condition like diabetes or cancer, or the rule now that you can't charge somebody more just because they're a woman—all those reforms would go away for everybody, because that's part of Obamacare.

All the progress that we've made in controlling costs and improving how health care is delivered, progress that's helped hold growth in the price of health care to the slowest rate in fifty years—all that goes away. That's what repeal means. It would be bad for everybody. And the majority of Americans, even if they don't know that they're benefitting from Obamacare, don't want to see these benefits and protections taken away from their families now that they have them. I guarantee you there are people who right now think they hate Obamacare. And if somebody told them, all right, we're repealing it, but now your kid who is on your plan is no longer on your plan, or now you've got a preexisting condition and you can't buy health insurance, they'd be shocked. They [would say]—what do you mean?

So, repeal is not the answer. Here is what we can do instead to actually make the Affordable Care Act work even better than it's working right now. And I've already mentioned one.

Florida and every state should expand Medicaid. Cover more people. It's easy to do, and it could be done right now. You'd cover four million more Americans, help drive down premiums for folks who buy insurance through the marketplace. And, by the way, because the federal government pays for almost all of this expansion, you can't use as an excuse that, well, the state can't afford it, because the federal government is paying it. States like Louisiana that just expanded Medicaid—you had a Republican governor replaced by a Democratic governor. He said, I want that money. Expanded Medicaid, and found not only does it insure more people, but it's actually saved the state big money and makes people less dependent on expensive emergency room care. So that's step number one.

Step number two. Since overall health care costs have turned out to be significantly lower than everyone expected since we passed Obamacare, since that's saved the federal government billions of dollars, we should use some of that money, some of those savings to now provide more tax credits for more middle-income families, for more young adults to help them buy insurance. It will make their premiums more affordable. And that's not just good for them, it's good for everybody. Because when more people are in the marketplace, everybody will benefit from lower premiums. Healthier people, younger people start joining the pool; premiums generally go down. That would be number two.

The third thing we should do is add what's called a public plan fallback to give folks more options in those places where there are just not enough insurers to compete. And that's especially important in some rural communities and rural states and counties. If you live in L.A. right now, then it's working fine. There are a lot of insurers because it's a big market; there are a lot of providers. But if you're in some remote areas, or you're near some small towns, it may be that the economics of it just don't work unless the government is providing an option to make it affordable. And, by the way, this is not complicated. Basically, you would just wait and see—if the private insurers are competing for business, then you don't have to trigger a public option. But if no private insurers are providing affordable insurance in an area, then the government would step in with a quality plan that people can afford.

And, by the way, this is not a radical idea. This idea is modeled on something that Republicans championed under George Bush for the Medicare Part D drug benefit program. It was fine when it was their idea. The fact that they're now opposed to it as some socialist scheme is not being consistent, it's being partisan.

And finally, we should continue to encourage innovation by the states. What the Affordable Care Act says is, here's how we propose you insure your populations, but you, the state, can figure out a different way to accomplish the same goal—providing affordable, comprehensive coverage for the same number of residents at the same cost—then go right ahead. There may be more than one way to skin a cat. Maybe you've got an idea we haven't thought of. Just show us, don't talk about it. Show us what the plan looks like.

Republicans who claim to care about your health insurance choices and your premiums, but then offer nothing and block commonsense solutions like the ones that I propose to improve them—that's not right. And my message to them has been and will continue to be: Work with us. Make the system better. Help the people you serve. We're open to good ideas, but they've got to be real ideas—not just slogans, not just votes to repeal. And they've got to pass basic muster. You can't say, well, if we just do—if we just plant some magic beans then everybody will have health insurance. No, we've got to have health care economists and experts look at it and see if the thing would actually work.

So that's where we are. Number one, Obamacare is helping millions of people right now. The uninsured rate has never been lower. It's helping everybody who already has health insurance, because it makes their policies better. Number two, there are still too many hardworking people who are not being reached by the law. Number three, if we tweak the program to reach those people who are not currently benefiting from the law, it will be good for them and it will be good for the country. Number four, if we repeal this law wholesale that will hurt the people who don't have coverage right now. It will hurt the twenty million who are already getting help through the law. And it will hurt the country as a whole.

So, this should be an easy choice. All it does—all it requires is putting aside ideology, and in good faith trying to implement the law of the land. And what we've learned, by the way, is that when governors and state legislators expand Medicaid for their citizens and they hold insurance companies accountable, and they're honest with uninsured people about their options, and they're working with us on outreach, then the marketplace works the way it's supposed to. And when they don't, the marketplaces tend to have more problems. And that shouldn't be surprising. If state leaders purposely try to make something not work, then it's not going to run as smoothly as if they were trying to make it work. Common sense. You don't even have to go to Miami-Dade to figure that out.

The point is, now is not the time to move backwards on health care reform. Now is the time to move forward. The problems that may have arisen from the Affordable Care Act is not because government is too involved in the process. The problem is, is that we have not reached everybody and pulled them in. And think about it. When one of these companies comes out with a new smartphone and it had a few bugs, what do they do? They fix it. They upgrade—unless it catches fire, then they pull it off the market. But you don't go back to using a rotary phone. You don't say, well, we're repealing smartphones—we're just going to do the dial-up thing. That's not what you do.

Well, the same basic principle applies here. We're not going to go back to discriminating against Americans with preexisting conditions. We're not going to go back to a time when peoples' coverage was dropped when they got sick. We're not going to go back to a situation where we're reinstating lifetime limits in the fine print so that you think you have insurance, and then you get really sick or your kid gets really sick, and you hit the limit that the insurance company set, and next thing you know they're not covering you anymore, and you got to figure out how you come up with another $100,000 or $200,000 to make sure that your child lives. We're not going to go back to that.

I hear Republicans in Congress object, and they'll say, no, no, no, no, we'll keep those parts of Obamacare that are popular; we'll just repeal everything else. Well, it turns out that the sum of those parts that are popular in Obamacare is Obamacare. It's just people don't always know it. And repealing it would make the majority of Americans worse off when it comes to health care.

And as I said, part of this is just—you know, health care is complicated. Think about this speech—it's been pretty long, and you're just, you're thinking, wow, I just want to take a picture with the president or something. So, it's hard to get people focused on the facts. And even reporters who have covered this stuff—and they do a good job; they're trying to follow all the debate. But a lot of times they just report, "Premium increases." And everybody thinks, wow, my insurance rates are going up, it must be Obama's fault—even though you don't get health insurance through Obamacare, you get it through your job, and even though your increases have gone up a lot slower. Or suddenly you're paying a bigger co-pay, and, ah, thanks Obama. Well, no, I had nothing to do with that.

So, part of it is [that] this is complicated, the way it gets reported. There's a lot of hysteria around anything that happens. And what we need to do is just focus on this very specific problem—how do we make sure that more people are getting coverage, and folks right now who are not getting tax credits, aren't getting Medicaid, how do we help them, how do we reach them. And we can do it.

Instead of repealing the law, I believe the next president and the next Congress should take what we've learned over the past six years and in a serious way analyze it, figure out what it is that needs to get done, and make the Affordable Care Act better and cover even more people. But understand, no president can do it alone. We will need Republicans in Congress and in state governments to act responsibly and put politics aside. Because I want to remind you, a lot of the Affordable Care Act is built on Republican ideas.

In fact, Bernie Sanders is still mad at me because we didn't get single-payer passed. Now, we couldn't get single-payer passed, and I wanted to make sure that we helped as many people as possible, given the political constraints. And so, we adopted a system that Republicans should like; it's based on a competitive, market-based system in which people have to a responsibility for themselves to buy insurance.

And maybe now that I'm leaving office, maybe Republicans can stop with the sixty-something repeal votes they've taken, and stop pretending that they have a serious alternative, and stop pretending that all the terrible things they said would happen have actually happened, when they have not, and just work with the next president to smooth out the kinks.

Because it turns out, no major social innovation in America has ever worked perfectly at the start. Social Security didn't. Its benefits were stingy at first. It left out a whole lot of Americans. The same was true for Medicare. The same was true for Medicaid. The same was true for the prescription drug law. But what happened was, every year, people of goodwill from both parties tried to make it better. And that's what we need to do right now.

And I promise, if Republicans have good ideas to provide more coverage for folks like Amanda, I will be all for it. I don't care whose idea it is, I just want it to work. They can even change the name of the law to ReaganCare. Or they can call it Paul Ryan Care. I don't care about credit, I just want it to work because I care about the American people and making sure they've got health insurance.

But that brings me to my final point, and that is change does not typically come from the top down, it always comes from the bottom up. The Affordable Care Act was passed because the American people mobilized, not just to get me elected, but to keep the pressure on me to actually do something about health care and to put pressure on members of Congress to do something about it. And that's how change happens in America. It doesn't happen on its own. It doesn't happen from on high. It happens from the bottom up. And breaking gridlock will come only when the American people demand it.

So that's why I'm here. Only you can break this stalemate, by educating the public on the benefits of the Affordable Care Act, and then pressing your elected officials to do the right thing and supporting elected officials who are doing the right things.

And this is one of the reasons why I'm so proud of what Miami-Dade College is doing, because it's making sure that students and faculty, and people throughout this community know about the law, know about how to sign up for health care, and then actually helps people sign up. And I'm incredibly proud of the leadership Joe Peña and the entire team in encouraging people to sign up.

Thanks to them, Miami-Dade has been hosting enrollment office hours and workshops, even on nights and weekends. Right here on the Wolfson campus, and on all the Miami-Dade campuses, you can go for a free one-on-one session where a trained expert can walk you through the process and answer any questions you have—and then help you sign up for health care right there and then. Joe says he doesn't have a conversation without making sure people know how to get covered. The more young and healthy people like you who do the smart thing and sign up, then the better it's going to work for everybody.

And the good news is, in a few days, you can do just that because open enrollment, the time when you can start signing up, begins on November 1. And you just need to go to HealthCare.gov, which works really well now.

And campuses will be competing to come up with the most creative ways to reach people and get them signed up—and I'm pretty sure that Miami-Dade can set the standard for the rest of the country.

So much has changed since I campaigned here in Miami eight Octobers ago. But one thing has not: this is more than just about health care. It's about the character of our country. It's about whether we look out for one another. It's about whether the wealthiest nation on earth is going to make sure that nobody suffers. Nobody loses everything they have saved, everything they have worked for because they're sick. You stood up for the idea that no American should have to go without the health care they need.

And it's still true today. And we've proven together that people who love this country can change it—twenty million people out there will testify. I get letters every day, just saying thank you because it's made a difference in their lives. And what [was] true then is true now. We still need you. Our work to expand opportunity to all and make our union more perfect is never finished—but the more we work, and organize, and advocate, and fight, the closer we get.

So, I hope you are going to be busy this November signing folks up. But more importantly, I hope, for all the young people here, you never stop working for a better America. And even though I won't be president, I'll keep working right alongside you.

Thank you, everybody. God bless you. God bless America. Thank you.

CHAPTER 13

Donald Trump

Inaugural Address

2017

We stand at the birth of a new millennium, ready to unlock the mysteries of space, to free the Earth from the miseries of disease, and to harness the industries and technologies of tomorrow. A new national pride will stir our souls, lift our sights, and heal our divisions.

D onald Trump was the unexpected winner of the 2016 presidential election. Polls, pundits, and the news media expected Hillary Clinton to win, and Trump's victory caught many by surprise. Trump appealed to voters who felt Washington had stopped protecting the interests of the American people and was no longer putting America first. Trump pledged to "Make America Great Again." The campaign season leading up to this inaugural address was particularly divisive with both candidates making personal attacks against the other.

Trump's inaugural address presents a promising moment in his presidency. He talks about uniting Americans, shared values, and how to restore American greatness at home and abroad. He promises to break the insider culture in Washington and to represent the interest of all Americans. With hindsight, we know that his language while in office, his policies, and his actions proved to be highly divisive, but he started the term with a strong message nonetheless.

During the Trump presidency, the nation saw the advent of the COVID-19 pandemic and the police killing of George Floyd. Although presidents are typically called upon to unify the nation in times of crisis, some of Trump's rhetoric and handling of issues proved to do the opposite, increasing the partisan divide instead. However, his inaugural address was not a prelude to this division. Trump started his presidency off on the right foot by speaking to America as a whole, trying to unite a nation that faced deep chasms after the 2016 election.

Chief Justice Roberts, President Carter, President Clinton, President Bush, President Obama, fellow Americans, and people of the world: thank you. We, the citizens of America, are now joined in a great national effort to rebuild our country and restore its promise for all of our people.

Together we will determine the course of America, and the world, for years to come. We will face challenges. We will confront hardships. But we will get the job done.

Every four years, we gather on these steps to carry out the orderly and peaceful transfer of power, and we are grateful to President Obama and First Lady Michelle Obama for their gracious aid throughout this transition. They have been magnificent.

Today's ceremony, however, has very special meaning, because today we are not merely transferring power from one administration to another, or from one party to another, but we are transferring power from Washington, D.C., and giving it back to you, the American people.

For too long, a small group in our nation's capital has reaped the rewards of government while the people have borne the cost. Washington flourished—but the people did not share in its wealth. Politicians prospered—but the jobs left, and the factories closed. The establishment protected itself, but not the citizens of our country. Their victories have not been your victories; their triumphs have not been your triumphs; and while they celebrated in our nation's capital, there was little to celebrate for struggling families all across our land.

That all changes—starting right here and right now, because this moment is your moment: It belongs to you. It belongs to everyone gathered here today, and everyone watching, all across America. This is your day. This is your celebration. And this, the United States of America, is your country.

What truly matters is not which party controls our government, but whether our government is controlled by the people. January 20th, 2017, will be remembered as the day the people became the rulers of this nation again. The forgotten men and women of our country will be forgotten no longer.

Everyone is listening to you now. You came by the tens of millions to become part of a historic movement the likes of which the world has never seen before. At the center of this movement is a crucial conviction: That a nation exists to serve its citizens.

Americans want great schools for their children, safe neighborhoods for their families, and good jobs for themselves. These are just and reasonable demands of a righteous public.

But for too many of our citizens, a different reality exists: Mothers and children trapped in poverty in our inner cities; rusted-out factories scattered like tombstones across the landscape of our nation; an education system, flush with cash, but which leaves our young and beautiful students deprived of all knowledge; and the crime and gangs and drugs that have stolen too many lives and robbed our country of so much unrealized potential.

This American carnage stops right here and stops right now. We are one nation—and their pain is our pain. Their dreams are our dreams; and their success will be our success. We share one heart, one home, and one glorious destiny.

The oath of office, I take today, is an oath of allegiance to all Americans. For many decades, we've enriched foreign industry at the expense of American industry, subsidized the armies of other countries while allowing for the very sad depletion of our military. We've defended other nation's borders while refusing to defend our own. And spent trillions and trillions of dollars overseas, while America's infrastructure has fallen into disrepair and decay. We've made other countries rich while the wealth, strength, and confidence of our country has disappeared over the horizon.

One by one, the factories shuttered and left our shores, with not even a thought about the millions upon millions of American workers that were left behind. The wealth of our middle class has been ripped from their homes and then redistributed all across the world. But that is the past. And now we are looking only to the future.

We, assembled here today, are issuing a new decree to be heard in every city, in every foreign capital, and in every hall of power. From this day forward: a new vision will govern our land. From this day forward, it's going to be only America First. Every decision on trade, on taxes, on immigration, on foreign affairs, will be made to benefit American workers and American families.

We must protect our borders from the ravages of other countries making our products, stealing our companies, and destroying our jobs. Protection will lead to great prosperity and strength. I will fight for you with every breath in my body—and I will never, ever let you down. America will start winning again, winning like never before.

We will bring back our jobs. We will bring back our borders. We will bring back our wealth, and we will bring back our dreams. We will build new roads, and highways, and bridges, and airports, and tunnels, and railways all across our wonderful nation. We will get our people off of welfare and back to work—rebuilding our country with American hands and American labor. We will follow two simple rules: Buy American and Hire American.

We will seek friendship and goodwill with the nations of the world—but we do so with the understanding that it is the right of all nations to put their own interests first. We do not seek to impose our way of life on anyone, but rather to let it shine as an example. We will shine for everyone to follow. We will reinforce old alliances and form new ones—and unite the civilized world against radical Islamic terrorism, which we will eradicate completely from the face of the Earth.

At the bedrock of our politics will be a total allegiance to the United States of America, and through our loyalty to our country, we will rediscover our loyalty to each other. When you open your heart to patriotism, there is no room for prejudice.

The Bible tells us, "How good and pleasant it is when God's people live together in unity." We must speak our minds openly, debate our disagreements, but always pursue solidarity. When America is united, America is totally unstoppable.

There should be no fear—we are protected, and we will always be protected. We will be protected by the great men and women of our military and law enforcement and, most importantly, we will be protected by God.

Finally, we must think big and dream even bigger. In America, we understand that a nation is only living as long as it is striving. We will no longer accept politicians who are all talk and no action—constantly complaining but never doing anything about it.

The time for empty talk is over. Now arrives the hour of action. Do not allow anyone to tell you that it cannot be done. No challenge can match the heart and fight and spirit of America. We will not fail. Our country will thrive and prosper again.

We stand at the birth of a new millennium, ready to unlock the mysteries of space, to free the Earth from the miseries of disease, and to harness the industries and technologies of tomorrow. A new national pride will stir our souls, lift our sights, and heal our divisions.

It's time to remember that old wisdom our soldiers will never forget: That whether we are black, or brown, or white, we all bleed the same red blood of patriots, we all enjoy the same glorious freedoms, and we all salute the same, great American flag. And whether a child is born in the urban sprawl of Detroit or the windswept plains of Nebraska, they look up at the same night sky, they fill their heart with the same dreams, and they are infused with the breath of life by the same almighty Creator.

So, to all Americans, in every city near and far, small and large, from mountain to mountain, from ocean to ocean, hear these words: You will never be ignored again. Your voice, your hopes, and your dreams will define our American destiny. And your courage and goodness and love, will forever guide us along the way.

Together, we will make America strong again. We will make America wealthy again. We will make America proud again. We will make America safe again. And yes, together, we will make America great again.

Thank you. God bless you. And God bless America.

CHAPTER 14

Jeffry Flake

Resignation and Condemnation
of Political Deadlock

2017

In this century, a new phrase has entered the language to describe the accommodation of a new and undesirable order— that phrase being "the new normal." But we must never adjust to the present coarseness of our national dialogue—with the tone set at the top. We must never regard as "normal" the regular and casual undermining of our democratic norms and ideals.

———————

J effry Flake is an accomplished Republican politician with a long career of public service. He represented Arizona in Congress for the first two decades of the twenty-first century—from 2001 to 2013 in the House of Representatives, and then from 2013 to 2019 in the Senate. With this background, he became well-versed in the functioning of government. Like many other civil servants during the Trump presidency, Flake grew tired of political deadlock, inflamed rhetoric, lack of respect for institutions, and diminishing congeniality throughout Washington and the nation at large. Flake felt that despite awareness of the overall situation, nothing was being done to change it. Under normal circumstances he would likely have run for reelection, but in 2017, he felt he had to stand on principle and announced that he would not seek a second term as senator. He used his resignation speech to bring the issues he was seeing to light.

In specific, this speech calls out the "personal attacks," "threats against principles, freedoms and institutions," "flagrant disregard for truth or decency," and "reckless provocations" among politicians on Capitol Hill, while also criticizing Trump for fostering such a climate. Flake claims that the "new normal," as he puts it, is undermining democratic ideals and suggests that politicians have to unite to prevent these problems from becoming more widespread.

The theme of this book is the missing center, an overall call for politicians to take the high road and govern in the interests of the majority of Americans, not the far fringe elements of their political parties. It is a call for a return to decency, to respecting opposition views, and to finding areas of consensus and compromise. Or, put another way, it is a call to the days Jeff Flake remembers, days when government functioned properly. By 2017, Flake felt that the United States was so far adrift that the Senate was not acting normally. Through his decision to not run for reelection, Flake put his country before himself. His speech received positive comments in the press and from members of both parties. He used the power of his office to command attention and to take a stand. It is evident today that Flake's commentary was accurate and, in the long run, we hope not in vain.

As a promising sign in a time of divided government that perhaps his message was heard, after stepping down from the Senate, Flake was later appointed U.S. ambassador to Turkey by Joe Biden, a position for which he received unanimous bipartisan approval in his 2021 Senate confirmation hearings.

Mr. President, I rise today to address a matter that has been much on my mind, at a moment when it seems that our democracy is more defined by our discord and our dysfunction than it is by our values and our principles. Let me begin by noting a somewhat obvious point that these offices that we hold are not ours to hold indefinitely. We are not here simply to mark time. Sustained incumbency is certainly not the point of seeking office. And there are times when we must risk our careers in favor of our principles. Now is such a time.

It must also be said that I rise today with no small measure of regret—regret, because of the state of our disunion, regret because of the disrepair and destructiveness of our politics, regret because of the indecency of our discourse, regret because of the coarseness of our leadership, regret for the compromise of our moral authority, and by "our," I mean all of our complicity in this alarming and dangerous state of affairs.

It is time for our complicity and our accommodation of the unacceptable to end. In this century, a new phrase has entered the language to describe the accommodation of a new and undesirable order, that phrase being "the new normal." But we must never adjust to the present coarseness of our national dialogue with the tone set at the top. We must never regard as "normal" the regular and casual undermining of our democratic norms and ideals. We must never meekly accept the daily sundering of our country, the personal attacks, the threats against principles, freedoms, and institutions, the flagrant disregard for truth or decency, the reckless provocations, most often for the pettiest and most personal reasons, reasons having nothing whatsoever to do with the fortunes of the people that we have all been elected to serve. None of these appalling features of our current politics should ever be regarded as normal. We must never allow ourselves to lapse into thinking that this is just the way things are now. If we simply become inured to this condition, thinking that this is just politics as usual, then heaven help us.

Without fear of the consequences and without consideration of the rules of what is politically safe or palatable, we must stop pretending that the degradation of our politics and the conduct of some in our executive branch are normal. They are not normal. Reckless, outrageous, and undignified behavior has become excused and countenanced as "telling it like it is," when it is actually just reckless, outrageous, and undignified.

When such behavior emanates from the top of our government, it is something else. It is dangerous to a democracy. Such behavior does not project strength, because our strength comes from our values. It instead projects a corruption of the spirit, and weakness.

It is often said that children are watching. Well, they are. And what are we going to do about that? When the next generation asks us, "Why didn't you do something? Why didn't you speak up?"—what are we going to say? Mr. President, I rise today to say "Enough."

We must dedicate ourselves to making sure that the anomalous never becomes normal. With respect and humility, I must say that we have fooled ourselves for long enough that a pivot to governing is right around the corner, a return to civility and stability right behind it. We know better than that. By now, we all know better than that.

Here, today, I stand to say that we would better serve the country and better fulfill the obligations under the

Constitution by adhering to our Article I "old normal"—
Mr. Madison's doctrine of the separation of powers. This
genius innovation, which affirms Madison's status as a
true visionary and for which Madison argued in Federalist
51, held that the equal branches of our government
would balance and counteract each other when necessary.
"Ambition counteracts ambition," he wrote. But what happens if ambition fails to counteract ambition? What happens if stability fails to assert itself in the face of chaos and
instability? If decency fails to call out indecency?

Were the shoe on the other foot, would we Republicans
meekly accept such behavior on display from dominant
Democrats? Of course not, and we would be wrong if we
did.

When we remain silent and fail to act when we know
that that silence and inaction is the wrong thing to do
because of political considerations, because we might make
enemies, because we might alienate the base, because we
might provoke a primary challenge, because ad infinitum,
ad nauseum, when we succumb to those considerations in
spite of what should be greater considerations and impera-
tives in defense of the institutions of our liberty, then we
dishonor our principles and forsake our obligations. Those
things are far more important than politics.

Now, I am aware that more politically savvy people
than I caution against such talk. I am aware that there is
a segment of my party that believes that anything short
of complete and unquestioning loyalty to a president who
belongs to my party is unacceptable and suspect. If I have
been critical, it is not because I relish criticizing the behavior of the president of the United States. If I have been
critical, it is because I believe that it is my obligation to do
so, as a matter of duty and conscience.

The notion that one should stay silent as the norms and values that keep America strong are undermined and as the alliances and agreements that ensure the stability of the entire world are routinely threatened by the level of thought that goes into 140 characters, the notion that one should say and do nothing in the face of such mercurial behavior is ahistoric and, I believe, profoundly misguided.

A Republican president named Roosevelt had this to say about the president and a citizen's relationship to the office:

> *The President is merely the most important among a large number of public servants. He should be supported or opposed exactly to the degree which is warranted by his good conduct or bad conduct, his efficiency or inefficiency in rendering loyal, able, and disinterested service to the nation as a whole.*
>
> *Therefore, it is absolutely necessary that there should be full liberty to tell the truth about his acts, and this means that it is exactly as necessary to blame him when he does wrong as to praise him when he does right. Any other attitude in an American citizen is both base and servile.*
>
> *To announce that there must be no criticism of the President, or that we are to stand by the President, right or wrong, is not only unpatriotic and servile, but is morally treasonable to the American public.*

Acting on conscience and principle is the manner in which we express our moral selves, and as such, loyalty to conscience and principle should supersede loyalty to any man or party.

We can all be forgiven for failing in that measure from time to time. I certainly put myself at the top of the list of those who fall short in that regard. I am holier-than-none.

But too often, we rush not to salvage principle but to forgive and excuse our failures so that we might accommodate them and go right on failing until the accommodation itself becomes our principle.

In that way and over time, we can justify almost any behavior and sacrifice almost any principle. I am afraid that is where we now find ourselves.

When a leader correctly identifies real hurt and insecurity in our country and instead of addressing it goes looking for someone to blame, there is perhaps nothing more devastating to a pluralistic society. Leadership knows that most often a good place to start in assigning blame is to first look somewhat closer to home. Leadership knows where the buck stops, humility helps, character counts.

Leadership does not knowingly encourage or feed ugly and debased appetites in us. Leadership lives by the American creed, "E Pluribus Unum"—"From many, one." American leadership looks to the world, and just as Lincoln did, sees the family of man. Humanity is not a zero-sum game. When we have been at our most prosperous, we have also been at our most principled, and when we do well, the rest of the world also does well.

These articles of civic faith have been central to the American identity for as long as we have all been alive. They are our birthright and our obligation. We must guard them jealously and pass them on for as long as the calendar has days. To betray them, or to be unserious in their defense is a betrayal of the fundamental obligations of American leadership, and to behave as if they don't matter is simply not who we are.

Now the efficacy of American leadership around the globe has come into question. When the United States emerged from World War II, we contributed about half of the world's economic activity. It would have been easy to secure our dominance, keeping the countries that had been defeated or greatly weakened during the war in their place. We didn't do that. It would have been easy to focus inward. We resisted those impulses. Instead, we financed reconstruction of shattered countries and created international organizations and institutions that have helped provide security and foster prosperity around the world for more than seventy years.

Now, it seems that we, the architects of this visionary rules-based world order that has brought so much freedom and prosperity, are the ones most eager to abandon it. The implications of this abandonment are profound, and the beneficiaries of this rather radical departure in the American approach to the world are the ideological enemies of our values.

Despotism loves a vacuum, and our allies are now looking elsewhere for leadership. Why are they doing this? None of this is normal. And what do we as United States Senators have to say about it? The principles that underlie our politics, the values of our founding, are too vital to our identity and to our survival to allow them to be compromised by the requirements of politics because politics can make us silent when we should speak, and silence can equal complicity.

I have children and grandchildren to answer to, and so, Mr. President, I will not be complicit or silent. I have decided that I will be better able to represent the people of Arizona and to better serve my country and my conscience by freeing myself from the political considerations that consume far too much bandwidth and would cause me to compromise far too many principles.

To that end, I am announcing today that my service in the Senate will conclude at the end of my term in early January 2019. It is clear, at this moment, that a traditional conservative who believes in limited government and free markets, who is devoted to free trade, and who is pro-immigration has a narrower and narrower path to nomination in the Republican party—the party that for so long has defined itself by belief in those things.

It is also clear to me for the moment we have given in or given up on those core principles in favor of the more viscerally satisfying anger and resentment. To be clear, the anger and resentment that the people feel at the royal mess we have created are justified. But anger and resentment are not a governing philosophy.

There is an undeniable potency to a populist appeal, but mischaracterizing or misunderstanding our problems and giving in to the impulse to scapegoat and belittle threatens to turn us into a fearful, backward-looking people. In the case of the Republican party, those things also threaten to turn us into a fearful, backward-looking minority party.

We were not made great as a country by indulging or even exalting our worst impulses, turning against ourselves, glorying in the things which divide us, and calling fake things true and true things fake, and we did not become the beacon of freedom in the darkest corners of the world by flouting our institutions and failing to understand just how hard-won and vulnerable they are.

This spell will eventually break. That is my belief. We will return to ourselves once more, and I say the sooner the better because to have a healthy government we must have healthy and functioning parties. We must respect each other again in an atmosphere of shared facts and shared values, comity and good faith. We must argue our positions fervently, and never be afraid to compromise. We must assume the best of our fellow man and always look for the good. Until that day comes, we must be unafraid to stand up and speak out as if our country depends on it because it does.

I plan to spend the remaining fourteen months of my senate term doing just that. Mr. President, the graveyard is full of indispensable men and women. None of us here is indispensable, nor were even the great figures from history who toiled at these very desks in this very chamber to shape this country that we have inherited. What is indispensable are the values that they consecrated in Philadelphia and in this place—values which have endured and will endure for so long as men and women wish to remain free. What is indispensable is what we do here in defense of those values. A political career doesn't mean much if we are complicit in undermining those values.

I thank my colleagues for indulging me here today, and will close by borrowing the words of President Lincoln, who knew more about healing enmity and preserving our founding values than any other American who has ever lived. His words from his first inaugural were a prayer in his time, and are no less so in ours:

> We are not enemies, but friends. We must not be enemies. Though passion may have strained, it must not break our bonds of affection. The mystic chords of memory will swell when again touched, as surely they will be, by the better angels of our nature.

Thank you, Mr. President. I yield the floor.

CHAPTER 15

Donald Trump

The COVID-19 Vaccine Release

2020

The tremendous progress that we've made is a testament to what our nation is capable of. When America is faced with a challenge, we come through—and we always come through—to overcome every hardship and surmount every obstacle.

December 2020 marked a turning point in the world's reaction to the COVID-19 pandemic with the official rollout of vaccines to reduce the impact of the virus. Never before in history had a vaccine to a new pathogen been developed so quickly, and the launch offered the promise of a return to normalcy.

To facilitate the vaccines and their rollout to all who wanted them, President Trump signed an executive order marshaling the government's resources. While Trump speaks in a more casual and unscripted tone than other speeches in this book, the successful combination of government resources with private industry expertise was momentous. America has long been known for innovation and its role in solving global problems. This speech identifies how: the public and private sectors joining together to accomplish great things.

Government at its best is focused on solving society's most complex problems. Operation Warp Speed's approach, funding research at multiple labs each independently working on a common goal, was an intelligent strategy that increased the probability of success. This process enabled the development of different vaccine formulations against COVID-19 and paved the way for private-sector pharmaceutical manufacturing facilities to make the new vaccines and distribute them via private-sector freight companies in record time.

While there is much societal and political disagreement about the best way to manage the COVID-19 pandemic, the notion that the government could respond to the needs of its citizenry, provide a tool to protect vulnerable populations, and marshal ingenuity, are paradigms for global leadership.

I'm honored to welcome doctors, scientists, industry executives, and state and local leaders to our historic Operation Warp Speed Vaccine Summit. It's been some journey for all of us. It's been an incredible success.

We're grateful to be joined by Vice President Mike Pence, who has done an absolutely incredible job on the Coronavirus Task Force. . . .

We're here to discuss a monumental national achievement. From the instant the coronavirus invaded our shores, we raced into action to develop a safe and effective vaccine at breakneck speed. It would normally take five years, six years, seven years, or even more. In order to achieve this goal, we harnessed the full power of government, the genius of American scientists, and the might of American industry to save millions and millions of lives all over the world. We're just days away from authorization from the FDA, and we're pushing them hard, at which point we will immediately begin mass distribution.

Before Operation Warp Speed, the typical time frame for development and approval, as you know, could be infinity. And we were very, very happy that we were able to get things done at a level that nobody has ever seen before. The gold standard vaccine has been done in less than nine months.

On behalf of the entire nation, I want to thank everyone here today who has been involved in this extraordinary American initiative. . . .

My administration provided a total of $14 billion to accelerate vaccine development and to manufacture all of the top candidates in advance—long in advance.

As a result of this unprecedented investment, we are exceedingly proud that both Pfizer and Moderna have announced that their vaccines are approximately 95 percent effective, which is a number that nobody expected to be able to get to, far exceeding anything that really we— that anybody—thought. We went out and we said, "What do you think a maximum would be?" And I think doctors—we all came to the conclusion that something like that would be really incredible.

And we have other candidates looking right now. We have some big ones that we're going to be announcing very soon. We have some companies—great, great companies out there you all know about: Johnson & Johnson and— and others. And they're all coming in, and they're coming in very quickly. We expect to have some news on that very shortly. And we have worked very well with the companies, but if for any reason we have any problems, we will be instituting the Defense Production Act, and we will make sure that we don't have any problems for very long. We've instituted it before.

Two additional companies, AstraZeneca and Johnson & Johnson—as you know, the Johnson & Johnson is a one-dose, one-shot vaccine, so we're going to see how that works. That would be very helpful if that all came out, and I think it probably will. Also, they're showing tremendous—tremendous promise, all of them.

We're very hopeful that the FDA will authorize the Pfizer vaccine within days. We got to get it moving. And the Moderna vaccine almost immediately thereafter. Large numbers of tests and samples have been done, so hopefully that'll go very quickly.

If authorized, tens of millions of vaccine doses will be available this month. And we'll get it distributed very quickly. We have that all set. And hundreds of millions more will quickly follow.

Every American who wants the vaccine will be able to get the vaccine. And we think by spring we're going to be in a position that nobody would have believed possible just a few months ago. . . . They say it's somewhat of a miracle, and I think that's true.

The plan we put forward prioritizes the elderly and patients with underlying conditions, as well as health-care workers and first responders.

The ultimate decision rests with the governors of the various states—and I hope the governors make wise decisions—who will decide where the vaccines will go in their state and who will get them first. We urge the governors to put America's seniors first, and also, I think those who work with seniors . . . and doctors, nurses, first responders, et cetera.

This will quickly and dramatically reduce deaths and hospitalizations. And within a short period of time, I think we want to get back to normal. A very standard phrase. We want to just get back to normal, get back to where we were a little more than nine months ago. We were doing incredibly. And in many respects, we're still doing incredibly with our stock markets and everything else, which are hitting all new highs.

We've already finalized a partnership with Walgreens and CVS, whose executives join us today. Thank you very much for being here. Thank you very much. We appreciate it very much. And they will deliver vaccines directly to nursing homes as soon as the states request that they do so.

Later today, General Gus Perna will outline the detailed plan to rapidly distribute the vaccine to every state, territory, and tribe. States have designated over fifty thousand sites that will receive the vaccine. We've worked very closely with the states. Actually, we've had very good relationships with the governors—I almost think all of the governors—at least in those conference calls that are somewhat secret, other than sometimes on occasion, Mike, the press will break in, which is fine too.

It's amazing how you leave those rooms and about ten seconds later—there wasn't even time for a leak—they were on the call. But that's all right. So you assume that. You always assume that. But they'll be going through pharmacies, hospitals, health-care providers.

Through our partnership with FedEx, UPS, and McKesson, we'll ship doses from warehouses directly to the designated sites. And we're thrilled to be joined by representatives of those really great American companies. Those companies have worked with us, and they've been incredible to work with. . . .

You saw that very few people thought that this was possible. Of course, they'll be saying now, "We always told you it was so." But we have them saying a little bit different.

But it has been incredible. And it will end the pandemic. It will end the pandemic. And we're working with other nations. As you see actually by looking at your screen today, we're working very closely with other nations also to get the vaccines out to other nations. And that's very important. We work with the world. We're working with the world. We have great companies, and we're working with the world.

In just a few minutes, I'll sign an executive order to ensure that the United States government prioritizes the getting out of the vaccine to American citizens before sending it to other nations.

Now, if necessary, I told you, we'll invoke the Defense Production Act, but we don't think it will be necessary. If it is—it's a very powerful act, as you know, because we've used it very, very successfully.

While we begin to swiftly deploy the vaccine, we'll continue to expand the availability of groundbreaking therapies. Since April, advances in treatments have already helped reduce the mortality rate by 85 percent. Think of that: 85 percent. It's an incredible number.

I've delivered on my solemn promise to make the antibody treatments—they're brilliant; they're highly successful—available to every American, and we're doing that free of cost, totally free of cost. So we're making them available, and they're available now. And if somebody gets sick, it works, where they go and they get treatment if that's what the doctors are prescribing. And it's been incredible, the success.

And when you hear 85 percent, that's some number. To me, that's a number that goes along with anything else, including the vaccines, when you think about it. As well as we've done with the vaccines, when you hear "85 percent," people—people find that one hard to believe. But you look at the stats, and you see what's happening.

And you look at other countries; they're having tremendous difficulties in Europe—tremendous. Beyond—relatively beyond what we're having. They're having them all over the world.

But this will vanquish the—the problem, this horrible scourge—as I call it, the "China virus," because that's where it came from.

The virus has really been looked at and studied all over the world, and our scientists, our industrial and economic mobilization has been like nobody else in the world could have done. And it's very important that we share that with others and other nations.

I've worked and invoked the Defense Production Act over one hundred times to manufacture essential supplies in the United States. Despite the grim projections from the media eight months ago, where they said this was impossible—they actually said—and you saw that a little bit, but I could give you two hours' worth of it. But they said it will never happen; you could never do it; it was a pipe dream. But we—we did something that nobody thought was possible.

And we also did it where no American who has needed a ventilator has been denied a ventilator. When we—when this first came out, we weren't equipped for that. Nobody was equipped for that. And we're now making ventilators. And we have all we need in this country, but we're sending them to countries all over the world. We're making thousands and thousands of ventilators a month.

The United States has also created the largest, most advanced, and most innovative testing program in the world by far. We've conducted over two hundred million tests. Think of that: two hundred million tests—more than all of the European Union combined. It's not even close.

Just ten months ago, none of these innovations even existed. The tremendous progress that we've made is a testament to what our nation is capable of. When America is faced with a challenge, we come through—and we always come through—to overcome every hardship and surmount every obstacle. And I think you'll be seeing that over the next few months; the numbers should skyrocket downward.

We are the most exceptional nation in the history of the world. Today, we're on the verge of another American medical miracle. And that's what people are saying. People that aren't necessarily big fans of Donald Trump are saying, "Whether you like him or not, this is one of the greatest miracles in the history of modern-day medicine" or any other medicine—any other age of medicine.

American companies were the first to produce a verifiably safe and effective vaccine. Together, we will defeat the virus, and we will soon end the pandemic, and we will save millions and millions of lives, both in our country and all over the world. And we've already started.

Thank you again to every person here today and for the incredible achievements that you've done. You're going to be very proud of this day, and you're going to be very proud of this period of time because nobody thought this was possible. Nobody thought it was even remotely possible to do what we've done in a period of less than nine months—something that—just not even thinkable.

And we took a lot of heat when we said this is our goal, and we, frankly, weren't even quite using the numbers that we used. We far exceeded what we thought. If we would have said "Sometime next year," I think most people would have said, "That would be great. That would be a miracle." But we did it long before sometime next year.

So now I want to ask several leaders who have been crucial in this effort to join me on stage as I sign the executive order to ensure that American citizens have first priority to receive American vaccines. And then we're going to be working with other countries all over the world, and I think we'll be able to start doing that almost immediately also, because we have millions of doses coming in.

So thank you very much. Thank you. It's a great honor.

CHAPTER 16

Joseph Biden

Inaugural Address

2021

That democracy and hope, truth and justice, did not die on our watch but thrived. That our America secured liberty at home and stood once again as a beacon to the world. That is what we owe our forebearers, one another, and generations to follow.

Joe Biden's inaugural address came at a particularly fraught time in American history. Biden was taking the Oath of Office amid Donald Trump's heated objections that the election results were illegitimate and just weeks after Trump's supporters stormed the Capitol Building on January 6.

A hallmark of American democracy since the founding of the nation has been the peaceful transition of power. Prior to 2020, there have been two notable presidential election disputes. The 1876 election of Republican Rutherford B. Hayes over Democrat Samuel Tilden was ultimately decided by a Congressionally appointed commission. In 2000, the election of George Bush over Al Gore was settled by the Supreme Court.

Twenty years later, President Biden spoke directly to the controversy surrounding Trump's delegitimization of the 2020 election. Never before in U.S. history had the transfer of power been so acrimonious. On top of that, Americans were still in the throes of the coronavirus pandemic and social distancing, uncertain when their lives would return to normal.

Like many presidents before him, Biden delivered a rousing inaugural address with the intent to heal the nation. "Few periods in our nation's history have been more challenging or difficult than the one we're in now," Biden acknowledges. He rises to the occasion by remaining optimistic in the face of adversity, and urges the American public to do the same.

Biden speaks of partisanship, and how we must come together across the aisle, a notion that he refers to as "unity." Unity is essentially what this book advocates, in the form of restoring civility to American politics. Unfortunately, Biden's term in office wasn't as uniting as the promise of his inaugural address. He suffered the lowest approval ratings of any modern president. His administration saw congressional gridlock, stark disagreements on the nation's priorities, and heated rhetoric both between and within political parties. That said, this speech is a prime example of how to inspire American citizens in the face of challenge and uncertainty. It is eloquently written, seeks to overcome the culture of divisiveness, and speaks to American greatness, both in the past and days ahead.

Chief Justice Roberts, Vice President Harris, Speaker Pelosi, Leader Schumer, Leader McConnell, Vice President Pence, distinguished guests, and my fellow Americans.

This is America's day. This is democracy's day. A day of history and hope. Of renewal and resolve. Through a crucible for the ages, America has been tested anew and America has risen to the challenge.

Today, we celebrate the triumph not of a candidate, but of a cause, the cause of democracy. The will of the people has been heard and the will of the people has been heeded. We have learned again that democracy is precious. Democracy is fragile. And at this hour, my friends, democracy has prevailed.

So now, on this hallowed ground where just days ago violence sought to shake this Capitol's very foundation, we come together as one nation, under God, indivisible, to carry out the peaceful transfer of power as we have for more than two centuries.

We look ahead in our uniquely American way—restless, bold, optimistic—and set our sights on the nation we know we can be and we must be.

I thank my predecessors of both parties for their presence here. I thank them from the bottom of my heart. You know the resilience of our Constitution and the strength of our nation. As does President Carter, who I spoke to last night but who cannot be with us today, but whom we salute for his lifetime of service.

I have just taken the sacred oath each of these patriots took—an oath first sworn by George Washington. But the American story depends not on any one of us, not on some of us, but on all of us. On "We the People" who seek a more perfect union. This is a great nation, and we are good people.

Over the centuries through storm and strife, in peace and in war, we have come so far. But we still have far to go. We will press forward with speed and urgency, for we have much to do in this winter of peril and possibility. Much to repair. Much to restore. Much to heal. Much to build. And much to gain.

Few periods in our nation's history have been more challenging or difficult than the one we're in now.

A once-in-a-century virus silently stalks in the country. It's taken as many lives in one year as America lost in all of World War II. Millions of jobs have been lost. Hundreds of thousands of businesses closed.

A cry for racial justice some four hundred years in the making moves us. The dream of justice for all will be deferred no longer. A cry for survival comes from the planet itself—a cry that can't be any more desperate or any more clear.

And now, a rise in political extremism, white supremacy, domestic terrorism that we must confront and we will defeat. To overcome these challenges—to restore the soul and to secure the future of America—requires more than words.

It requires that most elusive of things in a democracy: Unity. Unity. In another January in Washington, on New Year's Day 1863, Abraham Lincoln signed the Emancipation Proclamation. When he put pen to paper, the president said, "If my name ever goes down into history, it will be for this act and my whole soul is in it."

My whole soul is in it. Today, on this January day, my whole soul is in this: Bringing America together. Uniting our people. And uniting our nation. I ask every American to join me in this cause. Uniting to fight the common foes we face: Anger, resentment, hatred. Extremism, lawlessness, violence. Disease, joblessness, hopelessness. With unity we can do great things. Important things. We can right wrongs. We can put people to work in good jobs. We can teach our children in safe schools. We can overcome this deadly virus. We can reward work, rebuild the middle class, and make health care secure for all. We can deliver racial justice. We can make America, once again, the leading force for good in the world.

I know speaking of unity can sound to some like a foolish fantasy. I know the forces that divide us are deep and they are real. But I also know they are not new.

Our history has been a constant struggle between the American ideal that we are all created equal and the harsh, ugly reality that racism, nativism, fear, and demonization have long torn us apart. The battle is perennial. Victory is never assured.

Through the Civil War, the Great Depression, World War, 9/11, through struggle, sacrifice, and setbacks, our "better angels" have always prevailed. In each of these moments, enough of us came together to carry us all forward. And, we can do so now.

History, faith, and reason show the way, the way of unity. We can see each other not as adversaries but as neighbors. We can treat each other with dignity and respect. We can join forces, stop the shouting, and lower the temperature. For without unity, there is no peace, only bitterness and fury. No progress, only exhausting outrage. No nation, only a state of chaos.

This is our historic moment of crisis and challenge, and unity is the path forward. And, we must meet this moment as the United States of America. If we do that, I guarantee you, we will not fail.

We have never, ever, ever failed in America when we have acted together. And so today, at this time and in this place, let us start afresh. All of us. Let us listen to one another. Hear one another. See one another. Show respect to one another.

Politics need not be a raging fire destroying everything in its path. Every disagreement doesn't have to be a cause for total war. And, we must reject a culture in which facts themselves are manipulated and even manufactured.

My fellow Americans, we have to be different than this. America has to be better than this. And, I believe America is better than this. Just look around. Here we stand, in the shadow of a Capitol dome that was completed amid the Civil War, when the Union itself hung in the balance.

Yet we endured and we prevailed. Here we stand looking out to the great Mall where Dr. King spoke of his dream. Here we stand, where 108 years ago at another inaugural, thousands of protestors tried to block brave women from marching for the right to vote.

Today, we mark the swearing-in of the first woman in American history elected to national office—Vice President Kamala Harris. Don't tell me things can't change.

Here we stand across the Potomac from Arlington National Cemetery, where heroes who gave the last full measure of devotion rest in eternal peace.

And here we stand, just days after a riotous mob thought they could use violence to silence the will of the people, to stop the work of our democracy, and to drive us from this sacred ground.

That did not happen. It will never happen. Not today. Not tomorrow. Not ever.

To all those who supported our campaign, I am humbled by the faith you have placed in us. To all those who did not support us, let me say this: hear me out as we move forward. Take a measure of me and my heart. And if you still disagree, so be it.

That's democracy. That's America. The right to dissent peaceably, within the guardrails of our Republic, is perhaps our nation's greatest strength. Yet hear me clearly: disagreement must not lead to disunion.

And I pledge this to you: I will be a president for all Americans. I will fight as hard for those who did not support me as for those who did. Many centuries ago, Saint Augustine, a saint of my church, wrote that a people was a multitude defined by the common objects of their love. What are the common objects we love that define us as Americans? I think I know. Opportunity. Security. Liberty. Dignity. Respect. Honor. And, yes, the truth.

Recent weeks and months have taught us a painful lesson. There is a truth and there are lies. Lies told for power and for profit. And each of us has a duty and responsibility, as citizens, as Americans, and especially as leaders— leaders who have pledged to honor our Constitution and protect our nation—to defend the truth and to defeat the lies.

I understand that many Americans view the future with some fear and trepidation. I understand they worry about their jobs, about taking care of their families, about what comes next. I get it. But the answer is not to turn inward, to retreat into competing factions, distrusting those who don't look like you do, or worship the way you do, or don't get their news from the same sources you do.

We must end this uncivil war that pits red against blue, rural versus urban, conservative versus liberal. We can do this if we open our souls instead of hardening our hearts. If we show a little tolerance and humility. If we're willing to stand in the other person's shoes just for a moment.

Because here is the thing about life: There is no accounting for what fate will deal you. There are some days when we need a hand. There are other days when we're called on to lend one. This is how we must be with one another. And, if we are this way, our country will be stronger, more prosperous, more ready for the future.

My fellow Americans, in the work ahead of us, we will need each other. We will need all our strength to persevere through this dark winter. We are entering what may well be the toughest and deadliest period of the virus. We must set aside the politics and finally face this pandemic as one nation.

I promise you this: as the Bible says, "Weeping may endure for a night, but joy cometh in the morning." We will get through this, together. The world is watching today.

So here is my message to those beyond our borders: America has been tested and we have come out stronger for it. We will repair our alliances and engage with the world once again. Not to meet yesterday's challenges, but today's and tomorrow's.

We will lead not merely by the example of our power but the power of our example. We will be a strong and trusted partner for peace, progress, and security.

We have been through so much in this nation. And, in my first act as president, I would like to ask you to join me in a moment of silent prayer to remember all those we lost this past year to the pandemic.

To those 400,000 fellow Americans—mothers and fathers, husbands and wives, sons and daughters, friends, neighbors, and co-workers. We will honor them by becoming the people and nation we know we can and should be. Let us say a silent prayer for those who lost their lives, for those they left behind, and for our country. Amen.

This is a time of testing. We face an attack on democracy and on truth. A raging virus. Growing inequity. The sting of systemic racism. A climate in crisis. America's role in the world. Any one of these would be enough to challenge us in profound ways. But the fact is we face them all at once, presenting this nation with the gravest of responsibilities.

Now we must step up. All of us. It is a time for boldness, for there is so much to do. And, this is certain.

We will be judged, you and I, for how we resolve the cascading crises of our era. Will we rise to the occasion? Will we master this rare and difficult hour? Will we meet our obligations and pass along a new and better world for our children? I believe we must, and I believe we will.

And when we do, we will write the next chapter in the American story. . . . Let us add our own work and prayers to the unfolding story of our nation. If we do this, then when our days are through our children and our children's children will say of us they gave their best. They did their duty. They healed a broken land.

My fellow Americans, I close today where I began, with a sacred oath. Before God and all of you I give you my word. I will always level with you. I will defend the Constitution. I will defend our democracy. I will defend America. I will give my all in your service thinking not of power, but of possibilities. Not of personal interest, but of the public good. And together, we shall write an American story of hope, not fear. Of unity, not division. Of light, not darkness.

An American story of decency and dignity. Of love and healing. Of greatness and of goodness. May this be the story that guides us. The story that inspires us. The story that tells ages yet to come that we answered the call of history. We met the moment. That democracy and hope, truth and justice, did not die on our watch but thrived. That our America secured liberty at home and stood once again as a beacon to the world. That is what we owe our forebearers, one another, and generations to follow.

So, with purpose and resolve we turn to the tasks of our time. Sustained by faith. Driven by conviction. And, devoted to one another and to this country we love with all our hearts.

May God bless America and may God protect our troops. Thank you, America.

CHAPTER 17

Joseph Biden

One-Year Anniversary
of the January 6 Capitol Riot

2022

We will make sure the will of the people is heard; that the ballot prevails, not violence; that authority in this nation will always be peacefully transferred. I believe the power of the presidency and the purpose is to unite this nation, not divide it; to lift us up, not tear us apart; to be about us—about us, not about 'me.'

The January 6 Capitol Riot was perhaps one of the hardest tests America has faced. The United States was attacked at its literal Capitol—the heart of our democracy. Senators, representatives, law enforcement, staffers, and others who help keep America running were afraid for their lives. Five police officers died and over 150 were injured as a result of the riots. But ultimately the rule of law prevailed. The rioters were arrested and tried, new Capitol security measures were installed, and two weeks later the nation saw the peaceful transfer of power between presidents as Donald Trump left the White House and Joe Biden was inaugurated.

The events of January 6 illustrate the fragility of democracy and how fortunate America is to have a strong system of government. Never before in U.S. history had there not been an accepted transfer of power from one president to another. It has always been accepted in America that the citizens vote, elections are certified, one person steps down, and another takes the oath of office. This is true for presidents, governors, congressmen, judges, district attorneys, and local officials. There are procedures for disputing elections and mechanisms in place to settle disagreements through state law and Congressional action, as well as precedent for the involvement of the U.S. Supreme Court, as America saw in *Bush v. Gore* in 2000. The notion that a sitting U.S. president would refuse to leave office, threaten to call up the military to defend him, prosecute those opposed to him, and encourage his followers to storm the Capitol was unprecedented. This is the climate in which Biden took the oath of office. One year later, he delivered a moving address reflecting on the January 6 Riot.

It is interesting to compare this speech to Biden's Inaugural address one year earlier (chapter 16). Although the tones of the speeches are different, the messages are the same. Namely, that we the people prevailed. Biden reminds us how well the democratic experiment framed by the Founding Fathers has stood the test of time and become a model for other nations around the world. He speaks to the American experience, the richness of our culture, our openness to new ideas, and ultimately, how the will of the people is what guides our political leaders. Even though this speech was delivered during a dark time in U.S. affairs, Biden reminds us that America is resilient and that we are unified by a shared set of rules, laws, and values.

Madam Vice President, my fellow Americans: To state the obvious, one year ago today, in this sacred place, democracy was attacked—simply attacked. The will of the people was under assault. The Constitution—our Constitution— faced the gravest of threats.

Outnumbered and in the face of a brutal attack, the Capitol Police, the D.C. Metropolitan Police Department, the National Guard, and other brave law enforcement officials saved the rule of law.

Our democracy held. We the people endured. And we the people prevailed.

For the first time in our history, a president had not just lost an election, he tried to prevent the peaceful transfer of power as a violent mob breached the Capitol. But they failed. They failed. And on this day of remembrance, we must make sure that such an attack never, never happens again.

I'm speaking to you today from Statuary Hall in the United States Capitol. This is where the House of Representatives met for fifty years in the decades leading up to the Civil War. This is—on this floor is where a young congressman of Illinois, Abraham Lincoln, sat at desk 191. Above him—above us, over that door leading into the Rotunda—is a sculpture depicting Clio, the muse of history. In her hands, an open book in which she records the events taking place in this chamber below.

Clio stood watch over this hall one year ago today, as she has for more than two hundred years. She recorded what took place. The real history. The real facts. The real truth. The facts and the truth that Vice President Harris just shared and that you and I and the whole world saw with our own eyes.

The Bible tells us that we shall know the truth, and the truth shall make us free. We shall know the truth. Well, here is the God's truth about January 6th, 2021: Close your eyes. Go back to that day. What do you see? Rioters rampaging, waving for the first time inside this Capitol a Confederate flag that symbolized the cause to destroy America, to rip us apart. Even during the Civil War, that never, ever happened. But it happened here in 2021.

What else do you see? A mob breaking windows, kicking in doors, breaching the Capitol. American flags on poles being used as weapons, as spears. Fire extinguishers being thrown at the heads of police officers. A crowd that professes their love for law enforcement assaulted those police officers, dragged them, sprayed them, stomped on them. Over 140 police officers were injured.

We've all heard the police officers who were there that day testify to what happened. One officer called it, quote, a 'medieval' battle, and that he was more afraid that day than he was fighting the war in Iraq. They've repeatedly asked since that day: How dare anyone—anyone—diminish, belittle, or deny the hell they were put through?

We saw it with our own eyes. Rioters menaced these halls, threatening the life of the speaker of the house, literally erecting gallows to hang the vice president of the United States of America. But what did we not see? We didn't see a former president, who had just rallied the mob to attack—sitting in the private dining room off the Oval Office in the White House, watching it all on television and doing nothing for hours as police were assaulted, lives at risk, and the nation's capital under siege.

This wasn't a group of tourists. This was an armed insurrection. They weren't looking to uphold the will of the people. They were looking to deny the will of the people. They were looking to uphold—they weren't looking to uphold a free and fair election. They were looking to overturn one. They weren't looking to save the cause of America. They were looking to subvert the Constitution.

This isn't about being bogged down in the past. This is about making sure the past isn't buried. That's the only way forward. That's what great nations do. They don't bury the truth; they face up to it. Sounds like hyperbole, but that's the truth: they face up to it.

We are a great nation. My fellow Americans, in life, there's truth and, tragically, there are lies—lies conceived and spread for profit and power. We must be absolutely clear about what is true and what is a lie.

And here is the truth: The former president of the United States of America has created and spread a web of lies about the 2020 election. He's done so because he values power over principle, because he sees his own interests as more important than his country's interests and America's interests, and because his bruised ego matters more to him than our democracy or our Constitution.

He can't accept he lost, even though that's what ninety-three United States senators, his own attorney general, his own vice president, governors and state officials in every battleground state have all said: He lost. That's what eighty-one million of you did as you voted for a new way forward.

He has done what no president in American history—the history of this country—has ever, ever done: He refused to accept the results of an election and the will of the American people.

While some courageous men and women in the Republican Party are standing against it, trying to uphold the principles of that party, too many others are transforming that party into something else. They seem no longer to want to be the party—the party of Lincoln, Eisenhower, Reagan, the Bushes.

But whatever my other disagreements are with Republicans who support the rule of law and not the rule of a single man, I will always seek to work together with them to find shared solutions where possible. Because if we have a shared belief in democracy, then anything is possible—anything.

And so, at this moment, we must decide: What kind of nation are we going to be? Are we going to be a nation that accepts political violence as a norm? Are we going to be a nation where we allow partisan election officials to overturn the legally expressed will of the people? Are we going to be a nation that lives not by the light of the truth but in the shadow of lies?

We cannot allow ourselves to be that kind of nation. The way forward is to recognize the truth and to live by it. The Big Lie being told by the former president and many Republicans who fear his wrath is that the insurrection in this country actually took place on Election Day—November 3rd, 2020.

Think about that. Is that what you thought? Is that what you thought when you voted that day? Taking part in an insurrection? Is that what you thought you were doing? Or did you think you were carrying out your highest duty as a citizen and voting?

The former president and his supporters are trying to rewrite history. They want you to see Election Day as the day of insurrection and the riot that took place here on January 6th as the true expression of the will of the people. Can you think of a more twisted way to look at this country—to look at America? I cannot.

Here's the truth: The election of 2020 was the greatest demonstration of democracy in the history of this country. More of you voted in that election than have ever voted in all of American history. Over 150 million Americans went to the polls and voted that day in a pandemic—some at great risk to their lives. They should be applauded, not attacked.

Right now, in state after state, new laws are being written—not to protect the vote, but to deny it; not only to suppress the vote, but to subvert it; not to strengthen or protect our democracy, but because the former president lost. Instead of looking at the election results from 2020 and saying they need new ideas or better ideas to win more votes, the former president and his supporters have decided the only way for them to win is to suppress your vote and subvert our elections. It's wrong. It's undemocratic. And frankly, it's un-American.

The second Big Lie being told by the former president and his supporters is that the results of the election of 2020 can't be trusted. The truth is that no election—no election in American history has been more closely scrutinized or more carefully counted.

Every legal challenge questioning the results in every court in this country that could have been made was made and was rejected—often rejected by Republican-appointed judges, including judges appointed by the former president himself, from state courts to the United States Supreme Court.

Recounts were undertaken in state after state. Georgia—Georgia counted its results three times, with one recount by hand. Phony partisan audits were undertaken long after the election in several states. None changed the results. And in some of them, the irony is the margin of victory actually grew slightly.

So, let's speak plainly about what happened in 2020. Even before the first ballot was cast, the former president was preemptively sowing doubt about the election results. He built his lie over months. It wasn't based on any facts. He was just looking for an excuse—a pretext—to cover for the truth. He's not just a former president. He's a defeated former president—defeated by a margin of over seven million of your votes in a full and free and fair election.

There is simply zero proof the election results were inaccurate. In fact, in every venue where evidence had to be produced and an oath to tell the truth had to be taken, the former president failed to make his case.

Just think about this: The former president and his supporters have never been able to explain how they accept as accurate the other election results that took place on November 3rd—the elections for governor, United States Senate, the House of Representatives—elections in which they closed the gap in the House.

They challenge none of that. The president's name was first, then we went down the line—governors, senators, House of Representatives. Somehow, those results were accurate on the same ballot, but the presidential race was flawed?

And on the same ballot, the same day, cast by the same voters. The only difference: The former president didn't lose those races; he just lost the one that was his own.

Finally, the third Big Lie being told by a former president and his supporters is that the mob who sought to impose their will through violence are the nation's true patriots. Is that what you thought when you looked at the mob ransacking the Capitol, destroying property, literally defecating in the hallways, rifling through desks of senators and representatives, hunting down members of Congress? Patriots? Not in my view.

To me, the true patriots were the more than 150 [million] Americans who peacefully expressed their vote at the ballot box, the election workers who protected the integrity of the vote, and the heroes who defended this Capitol. You can't love your country only when you win. You can't obey the law only when it's convenient. You can't be patriotic when you embrace and enable lies.

Those who stormed this Capitol and those who instigated and incited and those who called on them to do so held a dagger at the throat of America—at American democracy. They didn't come here out of patriotism or principle. They came here in rage—not in service of America, but rather in service of one man. Those who incited the mob—the real plotters—who were desperate to deny the certification of the election and defy the will of the voters.

But their plot was foiled. Congressmen—Democrats and Republicans—stayed. Senators, representatives, staff—they finished their work the Constitution demanded. They honored their oath to defend the Constitution against all enemies, foreign and domestic.

Look, folks, now it's up to all of us—to "We the People"—to stand for the rule of law, to preserve the flame of democracy, to keep the promise of America alive. That promise is at risk, targeted by the forces that value brute strength over the sanctity of democracy, fear over hope, personal gain over public good.

Make no mistake about it: we're living at an inflection point in history. Both at home and abroad, we're engaged anew in a struggle between democracy and autocracy, between the aspirations of the many and the greed of the few, between the people's right of self-determination and self—the self-seeking autocrat.

From China to Russia and beyond, they're betting that democracy's days are numbered. They've actually told me democracy is too slow, too bogged down by division to succeed in today's rapidly changing, complicated world. And they're betting—they're betting America will become more like them and less like us. They're betting that America is a place for the autocrat, the dictator, the strongman.

I do not believe that. That is not who we are. That is not who we have ever been. And that is not who we should ever, ever be. Our Founding Fathers, as imperfect as they were, set in motion an experiment that changed the world—literally changed the world.

Here in America, the people would rule, power would be transferred peacefully—never at the tip of a spear or the barrel of a gun. And they committed to paper an idea that they couldn't live up to, but an idea that couldn't be constrained: Yes, in America all people are created equal.

We reject the view that if you succeed, I fail; if you get ahead, I fall behind; if I hold you down, I somehow lift myself up. The former president, who lies about this election, and the mob that attacked this Capitol could not be further away from the core American values. They want to rule or they will ruin—ruin what our country fought for at Lexington and Concord; at Gettysburg; at Omaha Beach; Seneca Falls; Selma, Alabama. What—and what we were fighting for: the right to vote, the right to govern ourselves, the right to determine our own destiny.

And with rights come responsibilities: the responsibility to see each other as neighbors—maybe we disagree with that neighbor, but they're not an adversary; the responsibility to accept defeat then get back in the arena and try again the next time to make your case; the responsibility to see that America is an idea—an idea that requires vigilant stewardship.

As we stand here today—one year since January 6th, 2021—the lies that drove the anger and madness we saw in this place, they have not abated. So, we have to be firm, resolute, and unyielding in our defense of the right to vote and to have that vote counted.

Some have already made the ultimate sacrifice in this sacred effort. Jill and I have mourned police officers in this Capitol Rotunda not once but twice in the wake of January 6th: once to honor Officer Brian Sicknick, who lost his life the day after the attack, and a second time to honor Officer Billy Evans, who lost his life defending this Capitol as well.

We think about the others who lost their lives and were injured and everyone living with the trauma of that day—from those defending this Capitol to members of Congress in both parties and their staffs, to reporters, cafeteria workers, custodial workers, and their families.

Don't kid yourself: The pain and scars from that day run deep. I said it many times and it's no more true or real than when we think about the events of January 6th: We are in a battle for the soul of America. A battle that, by the grace of God and the goodness and gracious—and greatness of this nation, we will win.

Believe me, I know how difficult democracy is. And I'm crystal clear about the threats America faces. But I also know that our darkest days can lead to light and hope.

From the death and destruction, as the vice president referenced, in Pearl Harbor came the triumph over the forces of fascism. From the brutality of Bloody Sunday on the Edmund Pettus Bridge came historic voting rights legislation. So, now let us step up, write the next chapter in American history where January 6th marks not the end of democracy, but the beginning of a renaissance of liberty and fair play.

I did not seek this fight brought to this Capitol one year ago today, but I will not shrink from it either. I will stand in this breach. I will defend this nation. And I will allow no one to place a dagger at the throat of our democracy.

We will make sure the will of the people is heard; that the ballot prevails, not violence; that authority in this nation will always be peacefully transferred. I believe the power of the presidency and the purpose is to unite this nation, not divide it; to lift us up, not tear us apart; to be about us—about us, not about "me."

Deep in the heart of America burns a flame lit almost 250 years ago—of liberty, freedom, and equality. This is not a land of kings or dictators or autocrats. We're a nation of laws; of order, not chaos; of peace, not violence. Here in America, the people rule through the ballot, and their will prevails. So, let us remember: Together, we're one nation, under God, indivisible; that today, tomorrow, and forever, at our best, we are the United States of America.

God bless you all. May God protect our troops. And may God bless those who stand watch over our democracy.

CHAPTER 18

Nancy Pelosi

Roe v. Wade Overturned

2022

As a woman, as a mother, as a grandmother, to see young girls now have fewer rights than their moms or even their grandmothers is something very sad for our country.

Nancy Pelosi was Speaker of the House when the Supreme Court voted in *Dobbs v. Jackson Women's Health Organization* to effectively overturn *Roe v. Wade* and no longer constitutionally guarantee a woman's right to have an abortion. The day the Supreme Court delivered this decision, many Americans were shocked that a matter which most had considered a settled precedent and protected right was stripped away. While the Religious Right and pro-lifers were exalted, the majority of Americans—84 percent—support a woman's personal right to choose in some or all circumstances. The *Dobbs* decision spoke to the missing center as it went against the views of most people and

199

felt like an affront to personal rights. The notion that a protection granted fifty years ago could be taken away rocked people's confidence in the Supreme Court and led many to question what other rights could be rolled back—not just in terms of reproductive freedoms, but also in civil rights or other accepted precedents that could be reversed by a new slate of justices.

In this speech, Pelosi argues that the newly conservative-leaning Supreme Court went against precedent by selectively applying their logic on a partisan issue. Just one day prior, they had ruled that federal law trumps state law on the right to bear arms. Yet on the issue of abortion, they ruled state law could take precedence over long-standing federal protections which most people had thought were permanently settled when *Roe v. Wade* was decided in 1973.

Pelosi speaks as a woman and as a legislator to voice her frustration and explains how she will lead legislation in Congress to protect individual reproductive freedom in face of the new ruling. Unlike State of the Union or major congressional addresses, which are often written months in advance, this speech is less polished than many in the book as it was written quickly, in reaction to the Supreme Court's decision that same morning. Despite the more casual delivery style, the words hit hard. Pelosi goes beyond abortion to discuss the dangers she sees from the new conservative majority Supreme Court. Pelosi feels she represents the views of the missing center as the Supreme Court decision was in opposition to views held by the majority of the electorate and went against prior legal precedent. She lambastes partisanship in the Supreme Court and seeks to overturn what she views as extremist positions in favor of policies generally supported by the majority of Americans.

There's no point in saying "good morning" because it certainly is not one. This morning, the radical Supreme

Court is eviscerating Americans' rights and endangering their health and safety. But Congress will continue to act to overcome this extremism and protect the American people. Today, the Republican-controlled Supreme Court has achieved their dark, extreme goal of ripping away a woman's right to make their own reproductive health decisions. Because of Donald Trump, Mitch McConnell, and the Republican Party—their supermajority on the Supreme Court—American women today have less freedom than their mothers. With *Roe* and their attempt to destroy it, radical Republicans are charging ahead with their crusade to criminalize health freedom.

In the Congress—be aware of this—the Republicans are plotting a nationwide abortion ban. They cannot be allowed to have a majority in the Congress to do that. But that's their goal. And if you read—and, again, we're all studying all this—but if you read what is very clear: one of the justices had his own statement. It's about contraception, in vitro fertilization, family planning. That is all what will spring from their decision that they made today.

Such a contradiction: yesterday, to say the states cannot make laws governing the constitutional right to bear arms. And today, they are saying the exact reverse: That the states can overturn a constitutional right—for fifty years a constitutional right—for a woman having the right to choose. The hypocrisy is raging, but the harm is endless. What this means to women is such an insult. It's a slap in the face to women about using their own judgment to make their own decisions about their reproductive freedom. And again, it goes—well, I always have said the termination of a pregnancy is just their opening act. It's just their front game. But behind it—and for years, I have seen in this Congress opposition to any family planning, domestic or global, when we have had those discussions and those debates and those votes on the floor of the House.

This is deadly serious. But we are not going to let this pass. A woman's right to choose—reproductive freedom—is on the ballot in November. We cannot allow them to take charge so that they can institute their goal, which is to criminalize reproductive freedom, to criminalize it. Right now, they are saying in states they can arrest doctors and all the rest. What is happening here? A woman's fundamental health decisions are her own to make in consultation with her doctor, her faith, her family—not some right-wing politicians that Donald Trump and Mitch McConnell packed the court with. While Republicans seek to punish and control women, Democrats will keep fighting ferociously to enshrine *Roe v. Wade* into the law of the land. This cruel ruling is outrageous and heart-wrenching. But make no mistake, again—it's all on the ballot in November.

The Supreme Court has ended a constitutional right. This [for] fifty years [has been] proclaimed [to be] a constitutional right. What happened today was historic in many respects. Historic in that it had not granted, recognized a constitutional right and then reversed it. This is a first and—again, just before, it imposed a constitutional right to allow for concealed weapons. How about those justices coming before the senators and saying that they respected stare decisis, the precedent of the court, that they respected the right of privacy in the Constitution of the United States? Did you hear that? Were they not telling the truth then?

Again—just getting to the gun issue, because really in preparation for this morning, I was really in an exalted state about what happened in the United States Senate yesterday. Counterpoint to the dangerous decision of this Trumpian Supreme Court that they made yesterday—but a way to take us to, as the bill is called, community safety, the Bipartisan Safer Communities Act. Right now—and I'm going to have to leave momentarily, because we just finished voting on the rule. We will be debating the bill on the floor, and we expect a good bipartisan vote on it in the House.

We congratulate the Senate on the work that they have done and the timelines of it to be passed in the Senate in a strong bipartisan way on a day when the court made such a dangerous, dangerous decision. Many of our House Democrat proposals are included in this package: keep deadly weapons out of dangerous hands by encouraging states to establish extreme risk protection order laws (ERPO), otherwise known as red flag laws; help put an end to straw purchases; close the "boyfriend loophole." So many good things are in there. And it is not everything that we wanted. We must keep moving toward background checks, but—universal background checks, which will save the most lives. But this will save lives.

And to listen to Lucy McBath and other family members of those who have lost their loved ones. This is a giant step forward. Maybe not so much a giant, but a strong step forward. And if it's good enough for them, then we rejoice in passing it.

As I say to members all the time with legislation, "do not judge it for what isn't in it, but respect it for what is." And there is much to be respected in this legislation.

On a happier note, yesterday we celebrated fifty years of Title IX, which has transformed equality and opportunity in our country. Are you familiar with the words of Title IX? Yesterday, we had Billie Jean King here, once

again, celebrating Title IX, unveiling a portrait of Patsy
Mink, who was the author in the House, working with
Birch Bayh in the Senate, to make this the law of the land.
And this is what it says:

> No person in the United States shall, on the basis of
> sex, be excluded from participation in, be denied the
> benefits of, or be subjected to discrimination under any
> education program or activity receiving federal finan-
> cial assistance.

Again, in honor of this anniversary, we unveiled a portrait
which will hang in the halls. It's about our Firsts . . . she's
actually the first woman of color to serve in the Congress.
So, she's honored for her first, but also for what she accomplished. We already have a painting of Shirley Chisholm,
the first African American woman, and for her many
accomplishments here. And, of course, Jeannette Rankin,
the first woman ever to serve in the Congress. That's our
"Firsts" series . . . .

I am personally overwhelmed by this decision. . . .
Clearly, we hoped that the Supreme Court would open
its eyes. But to see the chief justice side with this radical
agenda, it's just stunning.

And again, as a woman, as a mother, as a grandmother,
to see young girls now have fewer rights than their moms
or even their grandmothers is something very sad for our
country.

---

* *Portions of this speech not related to Supreme Court judgments and women's
rights were omitted.*

CHAPTER 19

Janet Yellen

American and Chinese
Economic and Political Relations

2023

Negotiating the contours of engagement between great powers is difficult. And the United States will never compromise on our security or principles. But we can find a way forward if China is also willing to play its part.

Tensions between the United States and China are currently at an all-time high. They manifest themselves economically, militarily, in domestic politics in both countries, and on a global stage. However, this is not a normal geopolitical rivalry, as both countries are among the other's top trading partners. The United States is dependent upon China for both raw materials and finished goods, while China is dependent upon American consumers and companies to keep its factories busy. The two nations have very different systems between democracy and communism, one embracing free-market principles and the other central planning. As two of the leading world powers the countries compete in, and clash over, their spheres of influence.

Although the United States and China often find themselves on opposing sides ideologically, it is of the utmost importance to both countries to avoid military conflict. In the following speech, Secretary of the Treasury Janet Yellen discusses the history of U.S.-Sino relations, showing how the nations' leading positions in world affairs have mutually benefited each other. Both countries' economies have flourished through trade and the exchange of ideas; however, as China has risen on the world stage, it has sought to assert itself by building coalitions opposed to Western leadership and is often criticized for violating human rights.

This speech does a brilliant job showing the complexity of the situation and the United States' willingness to work with China to lessen tensions. It is interesting to note that the speech was given by the Secretary of the Treasury, a high-ranking administration official, rather than President Joe Biden. In her role, Yellen speaks on behalf of the U.S. government, but gives the president distance from being seen as overly conciliatory toward China. Given the background of tariff wars, the status of Taiwan, and countless battles on the world stage, the Biden administration likely felt the need to demonstrate that despite their differences, an escalation of tensions is not America's desired course. In this speech, Yellen shows U.S. resolve to create a safer, equitable, and more prosperous climate for all nations to thrive without the "us vs. them" rhetoric of the Cold War. Yellen presents a forward-looking vision for peace and prosperity, rising above the political fray.

———

Good morning, everyone. Dean Steinberg, thank you for your kind introduction. And thank you for your service to our country. I'm grateful for your contributions—not only during your time in government but here at SAIS.

I'm particularly glad to be at this institution. SAIS has one of the oldest and most extensive China studies programs in the country. In 1979, the United States established full diplomatic relations with the People's Republic of China. Just two years after, your university leaders had their own talks with their Chinese counterparts. The goal was to see whether Johns Hopkins and Nanjing University could partner together to educate future leaders.

The result: the establishment of the Hopkins-Nanjing Center in 1986—one of the first Western academic programs in modern China. This collaboration has been tested by the realities and complexities of our bilateral relationship. But I believe the students on this campus have served as a reminder of the respect that the American and Chinese people have for each other. And they demonstrate that people around the world can learn from one another if we communicate openly and honestly—even and especially when we disagree.

Since I began my career, the relationship between the United States and China has undergone a significant evolution. In the 1970s, our relationship was defined by rapprochement and gradual normalization. I watched President Nixon make his famous journey to China in 1972. And I heard our two countries begin to speak to each other again after decades of silence. In the years that followed, I saw China choose to implement market reforms and open itself to the global economy, driving an impressive rise into the second-largest economy in the world. Its development was supported by assistance from the World Bank and other international economic institutions. And the U.S. Congress and successive administrations played a major role in supporting China's integration into global markets.

But in recent years, I've also seen China's decision to pivot away from market reforms toward a more state-driven approach that has undercut its neighbors and countries across the world. This has come as China is striking a more confrontational posture toward the United States and our allies and partners—not only in the Indo-Pacific but also in Europe and other regions.

Today, we are at a critical time. The world is confronting the largest land war in Europe since World War II—just as it recovers from a once-in-a-century pandemic. Debt challenges are mounting for low and middle-income countries. Some nations, including our own, have faced pressures on their economic and financial systems. And a U.N. report released last month indicates that the Earth is likely to cross a critical global warming threshold within the next decade—if no drastic action is taken.

Progress on these issues requires constructive engagement between the world's two largest economies. Yet our relationship is clearly at a tense moment.

So today, I would like to discuss our economic relationship with China. My goal is to be clear and honest: to cut through the noise and speak to this essential relationship based on sober realities.

The United States proceeds with confidence in its long-term economic strength. We remain the largest and most dynamic economy in the world. We also remain firm in our conviction to defend our values and national security. Within that context, we seek a constructive and fair economic relationship with China. Both countries need to be able to frankly discuss difficult issues. And we should work together, when possible, for the benefit of our countries and the world.

Our economic approach to China has three principal objectives.

First, we will secure our national security interests and those of our allies and partners, and we will protect human rights. We will clearly communicate to the PRC our concerns about its behavior. And we will not hesitate to defend our vital interests. Even as our targeted actions may have economic impacts, they are motivated solely by our concerns about our security and values. Our goal is not to use these tools to gain competitive economic advantage.

Second, we seek a healthy economic relationship with China: one that fosters growth and innovation in both countries. A growing China that plays by international rules is good for the United States and the world. Both countries can benefit from healthy competition in the economic sphere. But healthy economic competition—where both sides benefit—is only sustainable if that competition is fair. We will continue to partner with our allies to respond to China's unfair economic practices. And we will continue to make critical investments at home—while engaging with the world to advance our vision for an open, fair, and rules-based global economic order.

Third, we seek cooperation on the urgent global challenges of our day. Since last year's meeting between Presidents Biden and Xi, both countries have agreed to enhance communication around the macroeconomy and cooperation on issues like climate and debt distress. But more needs to be done. We call on China to follow through on its promise to work with us on these issues—not as a favor to us, but out of our joint duty and obligation to the world. Tackling these issues together will also advance the national interests of both of our countries.

Let me begin by discussing the state of our economies.

In recent years, many have seen conflict between the United States and China as increasingly inevitable. This was driven by fears, shared by some Americans, that the United States was in decline. And that China would imminently leapfrog us as the world's top economic power—leading to a clash between nations.

It's important to know this: Pronouncements of U.S. decline have been around for decades. But they have always been proven wrong. The United States has repeatedly demonstrated its ability to adapt and reinvent to face new challenges. This time will be no different—and the economic statistics show why.

Since the end of the Cold War, the American economy has grown faster than most other advanced economies. And over the past two years, we have mounted the strongest post-pandemic recovery among major advanced economies. Our unemployment rate is near historic lows. Real GDP per capita has reached an all-time high, and we have experienced the strongest two-year growth in new businesses on record.

This recovery is made possible by the strength of our economic fundamentals. Of course, this does not mean that our work is finished. Our top economic priority is to rein in inflation while protecting the economic gains of our recovery. A few weeks ago, the United States took decisive action to strengthen public confidence in the banking system after the failures of two regional institutions. The U.S. banking system remains sound, and we will take any necessary steps to ensure the United States continues to have the strongest and safest financial system in the world.

Over the past few decades, China has experienced an impressive economic rise. Between 1980 and 2010, China's economy grew by an average of 10 percent per year. This led to a truly remarkable feat: the rise of hundreds of millions of people out of poverty. China's rapid catch-up growth was fueled by its opening up to global trade and pursuit of market reforms.

But like many countries, China today faces its share of near-term headwinds. This includes vulnerabilities in its property sector, high youth unemployment, and weak household consumption. In the longer term, China faces structural challenges. Its population is aging, and its workforce is already declining. And it has experienced a sharp reduction in productivity growth—amid its turn toward economic nationalism and policies that substantially increase the government's intervention in the economy. None of these recent developments detract from China's progress or the hard work and talent of the Chinese people. But China's long-run growth rate seems likely to decline.

Of course, an economy's size is not the sole determinant of its strength. America is the largest economy in the world, but it also remains an unparalleled leader on a broad set of economic metrics—from wealth to technological innovation. U.S. GDP per capita is among the highest in the world and over five times as large as China's. More than resources or geography, our country's success can be attributed to our people, values, and institutions. American democracy, while not perfect, protects the free exchange of ideas and rule of law that is at the bedrock of sustainable growth. Our educational and scientific institutions lead the world. Our innovative culture is enriched by new immigrants, including those from China—enabling us to continue to generate world-class, cutting-edge products and industries.

Importantly, our economic power is amplified because we don't stand alone. America values our close friends and partners in every region of the world, including the Indo-Pacific. In the twenty-first century, no country in isolation can create a strong and sustainable economy for its people. That's why, under President Biden's leadership, we've sought to rebuild and reinvest in our relationships with other countries.

All this to say: China's economic growth need not be incompatible with U.S. economic leadership. The United States remains the most dynamic and prosperous economy in the world. We have no reason to fear healthy economic competition with any country.

There are many challenges before us. But the president and I believe that China and the United States can manage our economic relationship responsibly. We can work toward a future in which both countries share in and drive global economic progress. Whether we can reach this vision depends in large part on what both countries do in the next few years.

Let me speak to our first objective: securing our national security and protecting human rights. These are areas where we will not compromise.

As in all of our foreign relations, national security is of paramount importance in our relationship with China. For example, we have made clear that safeguarding certain technologies from the PRC's military and security apparatus is of vital national interest.

We have a broad suite of tools to achieve this aim. When necessary, we will take narrowly targeted actions. The U.S. government's actions can come in the form of export controls. They can include additions to an entity list that restricts access by those that provide support to the People's Liberation Army. The Treasury Department has sanctions authorities to address threats related to cybersecurity and China's military-civil fusion. We also carefully review foreign investments in the United States for national security risks and take necessary actions to address any such risks. And we are considering a program to restrict certain U.S. outbound investments in specific sensitive technologies with significant national security implications.

As we take these actions, let me be clear: these national security actions are not designed for us to gain a competitive economic advantage, or stifle China's economic and technological modernization. Even though these policies may have economic impacts, they are driven by straightforward national security considerations. We will not compromise on these concerns, even when they force trade-offs with our economic interests.

There are key principles that guide our national security actions in the economic sphere.

First, these actions will be narrowly scoped and targeted to clear objectives. They will be calibrated to mitigate spillovers into other areas. Second, it is vital that these tools are easily understood and enforceable. And they must be readily adaptable when circumstances change. Third, when possible, we will engage and coordinate with our allies and partners in the design and execution of our policies.

In addition, communication is essential to mitigating the risk of misunderstanding and unintended escalation. When we take national security actions, we will continue to outline our policy reasoning to other countries. We will listen and address concerns about unintended consequences.

Among our most pressing national security concerns is Russia's illegal and unprovoked war against Ukraine. In my visit to Kyiv, I saw firsthand the brutality of Russia's invasion. The Kremlin has bombed hospitals; destroyed cultural sites; attacked energy grids to cause widespread pain and suffering among civilians. Ending Russia's war is a moral imperative. It will save many innocent lives. As I've said, it is also the single best thing we can do for the global economy. To help end Russia's war, we have mounted the swiftest, most unified, and most ambitious multilateral sanctions regime in modern history. Our broad coalition of partners has also provided assistance to Ukraine so it can defend itself.

China's "no limits" partnership and support for Russia is a worrisome indication that it is not serious about ending the war. It is essential that China and other countries do not provide Russia with material support or assistance with sanctions evasion. We will continue to make the position of the United States extremely clear to Beijing and companies in its jurisdiction. The consequences of any violations would be severe.

Like national security, we will not compromise on the protection of human rights. This principle is foundational to how we engage with the world.

With our own eyes, the world has seen the PRC government escalate its repression at home. It has deployed technology to surveil and control the Chinese people—technology that it is now exporting to dozens of countries.

Human rights abuses violate the world's moral conscience. They also violate the foundational principles of the United Nations—which virtually every country, including China, has signed onto. The United States will continue to use our tools to disrupt and deter human rights abuses wherever they occur around the globe.

In public and in private with Beijing, the United States has raised serious concerns about the PRC government's abuses in Xinjiang, as well as in Hong Kong, Tibet, and other parts of China. And we have and will continue to take action. We have imposed sanctions on the PRC's regional officials and companies for a range of human rights abuses—from torture to arbitrary detention. And we are restricting imports of goods produced with forced labor in Xinjiang.

Across these actions, we are working in concert with our allies—knowing that we are more effective when we all go at it together.

As we protect our security interests and human rights values, we will also pursue our second objective: healthy economic engagement that benefits both countries.

Let's start with the obvious. The U.S. and China are the two largest economies in the world. And we are deeply integrated with one another. Overall trade between our countries reached over $700 billion in 2021. We trade more with China than with any countries other than Canada and Mexico. American firms have extensive operations in China. Hundreds of Chinese firms are listed on our stock exchanges, which are part of the deepest and most liquid capital markets in the world. According to the Nature Index, the United States and China are each other's most significant scientific collaborators. And China remains among the top sources for international students in the United States.

As I've said, the United States will assert ourselves when our vital interests are at stake. But we do not seek to "decouple" our economy from China's. A full separation of our economies would be disastrous for both countries. It would be destabilizing for the rest of the world. Rather, we know that the health of the Chinese and U.S. economies is closely linked. A growing China that plays by the rules can be beneficial for the United States. For instance, it can mean rising demand for U.S. products and services and more dynamic U.S. industries.

In April 2021, I delivered my first major international economic policy speech as Treasury Secretary. I said that "credibility abroad begins with credibility at home." At a basic level, America's ability to compete in the twenty-first century turns on the choices that Washington makes—not those that Beijing makes.

Our economic strategy is centered around investing in ourselves—not suppressing or containing any other economy.

In the two years since my speech, the United States has pursued an economic agenda that I call modern supply-side economics. Our policies are designed to expand the productive capacity of the American economy. That is, to raise the ceiling for what our economy can produce. To do so, President Biden has signed three historic bills into law. We've enacted the Bipartisan Infrastructure Law—our generation's most ambitious effort to modernize roads, bridges, and ports and broaden access to high-speed Internet. We've mounted a historic expansion of American semiconductor manufacturing through the CHIPS and Science Act. And we are making our nation's largest investment in clean energy with the Inflation Reduction Act. These actions have fortified U.S. strength in the industries of the future. And they are lifting our long-term economic outlook.

It's important to understand the nature of the healthy economic competition that the United States is pursuing. The United States does not seek competition that is winner-take-all. Instead, we believe that healthy economic competition with a fair set of rules can benefit both countries over time. A basic principle of economics is that sustained, repeated competition can lead to mutual improvement. Sports teams perform at a higher level when they consistently face top rivals. Firms produce better and cheaper goods when they compete for consumers. There is a world in which, as companies in the U.S. and China challenge each other, our economies can grow, standards of living can rise, and new innovations can bear fruit.

For example, China has benefited from American inventions like the personal computer and the MRI. In the same way, I believe that new scientific and medical developments from China can benefit Americans and the world—and spur us to undertake even more leading-edge research and innovation.

But this type of healthy competition is only sustainable if it is fair to both sides.

China has long used government support to help its firms gain market share at the expense of foreign competitors. But in recent years, its industrial policy has become more ambitious and complex. China has expanded support for its state-owned enterprises and domestic private firms to dominate foreign competitors. It has done so in traditional industrial sectors as well as emerging technologies. This strategy has been coupled with aggressive efforts to acquire new technological know-how and intellectual property—including through IP theft and other illicit means.

Government intervention can be justified in certain circumstances—such as to correct specific market failures. But China's government employs nonmarket tools at a much larger scale and breadth than other major economies. China also imposes numerous barriers to market access for American firms that do not exist for Chinese businesses in the United States. For example, Beijing has often required foreign firms to transfer proprietary technology to domestic ones—simply to do business in China. These limits on access to the Chinese market tilt the playing field in favor of Chinese firms. Further, we are concerned about a recent uptick in coercive actions targeting U.S. firms, which comes at the same moment that China states that it is reopening for foreign investment.

The actions of China's government have had dramatic implications for the location of global manufacturing activity. And they have harmed workers and firms in the U.S. and around the world.

In certain cases, China has also exploited its economic power to retaliate against and coerce vulnerable trading partners. For example, it has used boycotts of specific goods as punishment in response to diplomatic actions by other countries. China's pretext for these actions is often commercial. But its real goal is to impose consequences on choices that it dislikes—and to force sovereign governments to capitulate to its political demands.

The irony is that the open, fair, and rules-based global economy that the United States is calling for is the very same international order that helped make China's economic transformation possible. And the inefficiencies and vulnerabilities generated by China's unfair practices may end up hurting its own growth.

China's senior officials have repeatedly spoken about the importance of allowing markets to play a "decisive role" in resource allocation—including in a speech just earlier this year. It would be better for China and the world if Beijing were to actually shift policies in these directions and meet its own stated reform ambitions.

As we press China on its unfair economic practices, we will continue to take coordinated actions with our allies and partners in response. A top priority for President Biden is the resilience of our critical supply chains. In certain sectors, China's unfair economic practices have resulted in the over-concentration of the production of critical goods inside China. Under President Biden's leadership, we are not only investing in manufacturing at home. We are also pursuing a strategy called "friendshoring" that is aimed at mitigating vulnerabilities that can lead to supply disruptions. We are creating redundancies in our critical supply chains with the large number of trading partners that we can count on.

Of course, we know that the best way for us to strengthen the global economic order is to show the world that it works. Our investments in the international financial institutions and efforts to deepen our ties around the world are enabling more people to benefit from the international economic system. We are also accelerating our commitments in the developing world. For example, the United States and the rest of the G7 aim to mobilize $600 billion in high-quality infrastructure investments by 2027. Our focus is on projects that generate positive economic returns and foster sustainable debt for these countries. And when the international system needs updating, we will not hesitate to do so. The United States is working with shareholders to evolve the multilateral development banks to better combat today's pressing global challenges—like climate change, pandemics, and fragility and conflict.

As we set the terms of our economic engagement with China, we will also pursue our third objective: cooperation on major global challenges. It is important that we make progress on global issues regardless of our other disagreements. That's what the world needs from its two largest economies.

As a foundation, we must continue to develop steady lines of communication between our countries for macroeconomic and financial cooperation. Economic developments in the United States and China can quickly ripple through global financial markets and the broader economy. We must maintain a robust exchange of views about how we are responding to economic shocks. My conversations with Vice Premier Liu He and China's other senior officials have been a good start. I hope to build on them with my new counterpart.

Beyond the macroeconomy, there are two specific global priorities I'd like to highlight today: debt overhang and climate change. These issues can best be managed if both countries work together, and in concert with our allies and partners.

First, we must work together to help emerging markets and developing countries facing debt distress. The issue of global debt is not a bilateral issue between China and the United States. It is about responsible global leadership. China's status as the world's largest official bilateral creditor imposes on it the same inescapable set of responsibilities as those on other official bilateral creditors when debt cannot be fully repaid.

China's participation is essential to meaningful debt relief. But for too long, it has not moved in a comprehensive and timely manner. It has served as a roadblock to necessary action.

Earlier this year, I felt the urgency of debt relief firsthand during my visit to Zambia. Government and business leaders spoke to me about how Zambia's debt overhang has held back critical public and private investment and depressed economic development. But Zambia is not the only country in this situation. The IMF estimates that more than half of low-income countries are close to or already in debt distress.

The United States has had extensive discussions with Beijing about the need for speedy debt treatment. We welcome China's recent provision of specific and credible financing assurances for Sri Lanka, which has enabled the IMF to move forward with a program. But now, all of Sri Lanka's bilateral creditors—including China—will need to deliver debt treatments in line with their assurances in a timely manner. We continue to urge China's full participation to provide debt treatments in other cases in line with IMF parameters. This includes urgent cases like Zambia and Ghana.

Prompt action on debt is in China's interest. Delaying needed debt treatments raises the costs both for borrowers and creditors. It worsens borrowers' economic fundamentals and increases the amount of debt relief they will eventually need.

More broadly, there is considerable room for improvement in the international debt restructuring process. With the IMF and World Bank, we are working with a range of stakeholders to improve the Common Framework process for low-income countries and the debt treatment process more generally. As I heard from Zambian officials, solving these issues is a true test of multilateralism.

Second, we must work together to tackle long-standing global challenges that threaten us all. Climate change is at the top of that list. History shows us what our two countries can do: moments of climate cooperation between the United States and China have made global breakthroughs possible, including the Paris Agreement.

We have a joint responsibility to lead the way. China is the largest emitter of greenhouse gases, followed by the

United States. The U.S. will do its part. Over the past year, the United States has taken the boldest domestic climate action in our nation's history. Our investments put us on track to meet U.S. commitments under the Paris Agreement and achieve net-zero by 2050. And they will have positive spillovers for the world, including through reductions in the costs of clean energy technologies. We are also working abroad to help countries make a just energy transition to reduce their carbon emissions. These transitions will also help expand energy access and provide economic opportunity for impacted communities and workers.

We expect China to deliver on its commitments in our Joint Glasgow Declaration. This includes meeting mitigation targets and ending overseas financing of unabated coal-fired power plants. China should also support developing countries and emerging markets in their clean energy transitions. Further, we look forward to working together to boost private capital flows as cochairs of the G20 working group on sustainable finance.

We stand ready to work with China on the existential challenge of climate change. And we urge China to seriously engage with us and deliver on its commitments. The stakes are too high not to.

Some see the relationship between the U.S. and China through the frame of great power conflict: a zero-sum, bilateral contest where one must fall for the other to rise.

President Biden and I don't see it that way. We believe that the world is big enough for both of us. China and the United States can and need to find a way to live together and share in global prosperity. We can acknowledge our differences, defend our own interests, and compete fairly. Indeed, the United States will continue to proceed with confidence about the fundamental strength of the American economy and the skill of American workers. But as President Biden said, "we share a responsibility . . . to prevent competition from becoming anything ever near conflict."

Negotiating the contours of engagement between great powers is difficult. And the United States will never compromise on our security or principles. But we can find a way forward if China is also willing to play its part.

That's why I plan to travel to China at the appropriate time. My hope is to engage in an important and substantive dialogue on economic issues with my new Chinese government counterpart following the political transition in Beijing. I believe this dialogue can help lay the groundwork for responsibly managing our bilateral relationship and cooperating on areas of shared challenge to our nations and the world.

As you know, I am an economist by trade. Economics is popularly seen as a field concerning the structure and performance of entire economies. But at its most granular level, economics is much more foundational. It's the study of the choices that people make. Specifically, how people make choices under specific circumstances—of scarcity, of risk, and sometimes, of stress. And how choices by individuals and firms affect one another, and how they add up to a national or global picture.

In other words, an economy is just an aggregate of choices that people make.

The relationship between the United States and China is the same. Our path is not preordained, and it is not destined to be costly. The trajectory of this relationship is the aggregate of choices that all of us in these two great powers make over time—including when to cooperate, when to compete, and when to recognize that even amid our competition, we have a shared interest in peace and prosperity.

The United States believes that responsible economic relations between the U.S. and China is in the self-interest of our peoples. It is the hope and expectation of the world. And at this moment of challenge, I believe it must be the choice that both countries—the United States and China—make.

Thank you.

CHAPTER 20

Jerome Powell

Rising Interest Rates

2023

We remain committed to bringing inflation back down to our two percent goal and to keep longer-term inflation expectations well anchored. Reducing inflation is likely to require a period of below-trend growth and some softening of labor market conditions. Restoring price stability is essential to set the stage for achieving maximum employment and stable prices over the longer run.

Setting interest rates is one of the primary roles of central banks. They do so to heat up or slow down an economy, with inflation and unemployment being the core drivers which influence their decisions.

In mid-2021, as the United States was emerging from the COVID-19 pandemic, pent-up demand and blockages in global supply chains caused prices to rise, with annual inflation skyrocketing from

1.4 percent in 2020 to 7 percent in 2021. To address this, starting in March 2022 the Federal Reserve's Federal Open Market Committee began to raise the Federal funds rate to help bring down inflation.

These actions managed to slow the economy and prevented inflation from increasing at unsustainable rates. Although inflation subsided, high interest rates had ripple effects, including making home buying unaffordable for many and crimping consumer spending as people faced higher interest rates on debt. The rise in rates may have been a proximate cause of four commercial bank failures, or near-failures, in 2023: Signature Bank, Silicon Valley Bank, First Republic Bank, and Credit Suisse, which was acquired by UBS.

The chair of the board of governors of the Federal Reserve, commonly known as the chair of the Federal Reserve, is one of the most important positions in world financial markets. The media and banking sectors analyze every speech delivered by the chair in great detail. In this mid-2023 address directly following a series of bank insolvencies, Jerome Powell, chair of the Federal Reserve, announces that interest rates will be raised further. This speech captures a unique moment in time, as Americans hadn't encountered a period of such sustained inflation in decades. Much of the population grew up in an era of low interest rates with easy access to credit. These events reframed their financial assumptions.

Powell's position is supposed to be apolitical, and in this speech, he does not reference political parties. He speaks simply and clearly as an economist about his desire to control inflation, promote high levels of employment, prevent recession, and steer the United States toward a long-term healthy economy. Powell reaffirms his goal to bring inflation back to a target 2 percent rate and implies further action may be required in the future. If there is any government leader who speaks to the interests of the missing center in nonpartisan tones, Jerome Powell might be the best we have. The details of the speech demonstrate Powell's mastery of communicating complex topics in relatable terms.

———————

Good afternoon. Before discussing today's meeting, let me comment briefly on recent developments in the banking sector. Conditions in that sector have broadly improved since early March, and the U.S. banking system is sound and resilient. We will continue to monitor conditions in the sector. We are committed to learning the right lessons from this episode and will work to prevent events like these from happening again. As a first step in that process, last week we released Vice Chair for supervision Barr's review of the Federal Reserve's supervision and regulation of Silicon Valley Bank. The review's findings underscore the need to address our rules and supervisory practices to make for a stronger and more resilient banking system, and I am confident that we will do so.

From the perspective of monetary policy, our focus remains squarely on our dual mandate to promote maximum employment and stable prices for the American people. My colleagues and I understand the hardship that high inflation is causing, and we remain strongly committed to bringing inflation back down to our 2 percent goal. Price stability is the responsibility of the Federal Reserve. Without price stability, the economy does not work for anyone. In particular, without price stability, we will not achieve a sustained period of strong labor market conditions that benefit all.

Today, the FOMC raised its policy interest rate by ¼ percentage point. Since early last year, we have raised interest rates by a total of 5 percentage points in order to attain a stance of monetary policy that is sufficiently restrictive to return inflation to 2 percent over time. We are also continuing to reduce our securities holdings.

Looking ahead, we will take a data-dependent approach in determining the extent to which additional policy firming may be appropriate. I will have more to say about today's monetary policy actions after briefly reviewing economic developments.

The U.S. economy slowed significantly last year, with real GDP rising at a below-trend pace of 0.9 percent. The pace of economic growth in the first quarter of this year continued to be modest, at 1.1 percent, despite a pickup in consumer spending. Activity in the housing sector remains weak, largely reflecting higher mortgage rates. Higher interest rates and slower output growth also appear to be weighing on business fixed investment.

The labor market remains very tight. Over the first three months of the year, job gains averaged 345,000 jobs per month. The unemployment rate remained very low in March, at 3.5 percent. Even so, there are some signs that supply and demand in the labor market are coming back into better balance. The labor force participation rate has moved up in recent months, particularly for individuals aged twenty-five to fifty-four years. Nominal wage growth has shown some signs of easing, and job vacancies have declined so far this year. But overall, labor demand still substantially exceeds the supply of available workers.

Inflation remains well above our longer-run goal of 2 percent. Over the twelve months ending in March, total PCE prices rose 4.2 percent; excluding the volatile food and energy categories, core PCE prices rose 4.6 percent. Inflation has moderated somewhat since the middle of last year. Nonetheless, inflation pressures continue to run high, and the process of getting inflation back down to 2 percent has a long way to go. Despite elevated inflation, longer-term inflation expectations appear to remain well anchored, as reflected in a broad range of surveys of households, businesses, and forecasters, as well as measures from financial markets.

The Fed's monetary policy actions are guided by— by our mandate to promote maximum employment and stable prices for the American people. My colleagues and I are acutely aware that high inflation imposes significant hardship, as it erodes purchasing power, especially for those least able to meet the higher costs of essentials like food, housing, and transportation. We are highly attentive to the risks that high inflation pose to both sides of our mandate, and we are strongly committed to returning inflation to our 2 percent objective.

At today's meeting, the Committee raised the target range for the federal funds rate by ¼ percentage point, bringing the target range to 5 to 5¼ percent. And we're continuing to [carry out] the process of significantly reducing our securities holdings.

With today's action, we have raised interest rates by 5 percentage points in a little more than a year. We are seeing the effects of our policy tightening on demand in the most interest rate-sensitive sectors of the economy, particularly housing and investment. It will take time, however, for the full effects of monetary restraint to be realized, especially on inflation.

In addition, the economy is likely to face further headwinds from tighter credit conditions. Credit conditions had already been tightening over the past year or so in response to our policy actions and a softer economic outlook. But the strains that emerged in the banking sector in early March appear to be resulting in even tighter credit conditions for households and businesses. In turn, these tighter credit conditions are likely to weigh on economic activity, hiring, and inflation. The extent of these effects remains uncertain.

In light of these uncertain headwinds, along with the monetary policy restraint we have put in place, our future policy actions will depend on how events unfold. In determining the extent to which additional policy firming may be appropriate to return inflation to 2 percent over time, the committee will take into account the cumulative tightening of monetary policy, the lags with which monetary policy affects economic activity and inflation, and economic and financial developments. We will make that determination meeting by meeting, based on the totality of incoming data and their implications for the outlook for economic activity and inflation. And we are prepared to do more if greater monetary policy restraint is warranted.

We remain committed to bringing inflation back down to our 2 percent goal and to keep longer-term inflation expectations well anchored. Reducing inflation is likely to require a period of below-trend growth and some softening of labor market conditions. Restoring price stability is essential to set the stage for achieving maximum employment and stable prices over the longer run.

To conclude: we understand that our actions affect communities, families, and businesses across the country. Everything we do is in service to our public mission. We at the Fed will do everything we can to achieve our maximum-employment and price-stability goals. Thank you.

CHAPTER 21

Raphael Warnock

HEADWAY Act

2023

The idea here is real simple, and I'll repeat it again: When we center the people in our public policy, we get good results.

H ead Start is a program that provides access to preschool for low-income families. Data has shown that the earlier students start school, the greater their educational outcomes and likelihood to thrive as adults. Unfortunately, in the current environment, not all children are enrolled in pre-K. In 2021, only 42 percent of children between the ages of three and six were enrolled in preschool in the United States. The lowest participation percentages were among households with parents not in the labor force. The debate around this issue had been around for years and over time has become increasingly front of mind. By 2001, 61 percent of Americans supported free pre-K for all three- and four-year-olds.

Historically, preschools have mainly been private or parochial with parents paying their children's tuition. Although public preschools are beginning to be offered, it will take a long time for them to become standard practice in all places. As of the 2019–2020 academic year, just four states were able to accomplish the 70 percent enrollment benchmark set by the National Institute for Early Childhood Research for "universal" preschool. Many districts are resource constrained and cannot meet the full needs of their communities.

In this address, Senator Raphael Warnock takes a step toward improving public preschool access by introducing a bill that would address the staffing shortages many Head Start schools face. Teachers at preschools are required to be Child Development Associates, or CDAs. Warnock's Head Start Education and Development Workforce Advancement and Yield (HEADWAY) Act proposes allowing staff to earn their CDA while working in preschools as long as at least one fully certified educator accompanies the trainee in the classroom. This would make it significantly easier for Head Start programs to accommodate more students.

Warnock has long been a champion of providing funding to childcare providers, daycare centers, and education. This Act is especially important to Warnock because he was enrolled in Head Start as a child (the program was established in 1965) and credits some of his success to it.

In this speech, Warnock outlines a long-standing problem and advocates for remedies to fix it. He recognizes high education costs negatively impact families, eroding the societal benefits that come from socialization and learning. He strives to rise above Washington's political gridlock to find an issue that can attract bipartisan support to serve the needs of parents, children, and the nation, bringing us one step closer to a society where all families have access to early childhood education.

Hello and good afternoon to everybody here at the National Head Start Association's Fall Leadership Institute. I am so honored to be here today. . . . Before I begin, let's all give a big hand to the teachers, education professionals, and everybody here in this room and across the country who have worked so tirelessly to help shape a brighter future for our children.

You are heroes and deserve our admiration and respect. In a real sense, my life has been dedicated to the values everyone in this room holds dear: If we center the most vulnerable in our communities in our public policy, our country will be better off.

It really is that simple. I'm a proud Head Start alum, one of only two in the United States Senate. I like to say that I'm a product of good public policy, thanks to programs like Head Start—because only in this country is my story of being a kid who grew up in public housing to becoming a United States Senator possible.

And, in turn, I've spent my life trying to best serve the people, so that more folks from backgrounds like mine can access the bountiful opportunities available in this country. Like you, I've been engaged in the struggle, dedicated to public service and doing all I can to uplift every American.

A teacher of mine once told me, "Service is the rent you pay for the space you occupy," which is why I was inspired to a life in the ministry, and why I put my hat in the ring and ran for Senate to represent the great state of Georgia.

It's an incredible privilege to be entrusted by your neighbors to represent them and fight for them in Washington. And what I'm hearing from parents and families in my state is it is becoming even harder to get affordable, quality childcare, partly because of the lack of childcare professionals in their communities—which puts even more strain on families and our economy.

Look, as the father of two young kids, I know how important these early years are for development. And that is especially true for the kids you all serve—kids who were like me. But we know Head Start can make a massive difference in a young student's life.

From improving educational outcomes to promoting better social and behavioral development and increased nutrition access, there's a mountain of evidence that shows the good Head Start can have.

At the time of its inception in 1965, President Lyndon Johnson predicted that Head Start would be quote "one of the most constructive, and one of the most sensible, and also one of the most exciting programs that this nation has ever undertaken." President Johnson's prediction has more than proven itself to be true. Head Start is truly a magical and wonderful program.

In fact, just a few weeks ago, I got to see firsthand down in my hometown of Savannah how Head Start is continuing its mission to pave a path towards academic and life for so many kids and families across the nation. I know I have some Georgia Head Start friends in the audience right now—make some noise!

My visit in Savannah was a real-time demonstration of the work Head Start has been doing for decades that has changed the lives of more than thirty-eight million children. Think about that—thirty-eight million. Head Start's success has shown that poverty in this nation is a public policy choice. When our nation is serious about uplifting our fellow Americans who are less fortunate than us, the sky is the limit.

But right now, leaders in Washington aren't doing all we can to address the childcare crisis we're in and support

Head Start's magic and power, so you all can keep changing as many young lives as we need you to. Listen to these figures: 20 percent of Head Start and Early Head Start classrooms nationwide are currently closed; 19 percent of Head Start staff positions are vacant nationwide; and data from the Bureau of Labor Statistics shows that our childcare workforce numbers are still alarmingly below pre-pandemic levels.

This is a massive problem morally and for the strength of our nation—and you all are living with the consequences of this reality every day. We know investing in early childhood education is one of the most profound choices our country can make to stay competitive on the global stage. We cannot allow the gap between children from affluent backgrounds and children from low-income communities to grow.

That's why, as someone who wouldn't be where I am today without the tools and experience I had in Head Start, I'm particularly proud to announce today I am introducing a new bipartisan bill to start tackling this problem.

I'm offering my new HEADWAY Act with my partner Senator Mike Braun of Indiana to strengthen our childcare infrastructure by making it easier for early learning professionals to fill the shortages in our Early Head Start classrooms. My HEADWAY Act will address the shortage of early learning educators by allowing soon-to-be teachers to earn their required Child Development Associate credential while they teach in Early Head Start classrooms for kids ages zero to three, while retaining the requirement that at least one teacher in every classroom is fully credentialed with at least a CDA.

This bill will support Early Head Start learning professionals and give program directors the flexibility they need to respond to employment trends while still maintaining the high standards and professionalization of the field. And our bill will require mentorship for these early learning professionals to make sure they continue making progress toward earning their CDA.

This is good policy and it's good for our children. That's why I am doing this. And it's why I know NHSA will be with me in the trenches as we push to get this bill signed into law. Because you know when we help lift up kids from places like where I grew up, America is better off. When we strengthen Head Start, we are all better off.

When I was in Savannah, I saw how so many classrooms in Head Start aren't as full as they should be. As we want them to be. As we need them to be. I saw how vital it was to strengthen the childcare workforce pipeline. My visit in Savannah was just another reminder that early childhood development is the key not only for these young children, but also for their families, their communities, and for our economy.

In a real sense, my HEADWAY Act is aimed at giving our childcare educators—who are unsung heroes and the backbone of our education workforce—a "head start" in their careers. My bill will help ensure our Early Head Start classrooms are fully staffed, enabling Early Head Start to fulfill its commitment to providing high-quality early childhood education and laying the foundation for our kids' future success.

And it will open up desperately needed slots for students at every income level, providing more childcare opportunities for families. The idea here is real simple, and I'll repeat it again: When we center the people in our public policy, we get good results: from lowering the monthly costs of insulin; to pushing to boost mental health counseling for our students; to working to create more green energy jobs; to fighting for disaster relief for communities impacted by extreme weather; to keeping the government open and funded; and of course, protecting the sacred right [to] vote.

These all stem from the values I first learned in a Head Start classroom in Savannah. The work you are doing today and every day to strengthen and bolster early childhood education and Head Start programs across our country is making good on Dr. King's vision that we must all work to create a more beloved community.

Your tireless advocacy is setting the stage for a more generous and prosperous America, and I'm so honored to be your ally in this fight. Thank you so much for having me today and I hope you cause some good trouble on Capitol Hill advocating for what we all know is the right and smart thing to do. Thank you so much—keep the faith and keep looking up.

ACKNOWLEDGMENTS

I would like to express gratitude to my parents for teaching me so much and for all of their help and support. I could not be where I am in life without you. I enjoy our dinner conversations about how to make the world a better place, the importance of understanding the past, and always pushing me to add nuance, depth, and humility when advocating viewpoints. You taught me from an early age the values of hard work, compassion, and respecting others.

Thank you to my grandparents—Pop, Pop, Nonni, and Nana—for having imparted valuable life lessons and so many fun memories. All of you are an inspiration for myself and our family.

To my sister Elizabeth, I respect your intelligence, warmth, humor, and commitment to improving the world.

I wouldn't have been able to get this book done without Dr. Chandler, who helped me immensely in the brainstorming, research, writing, and editing processes. We had many conversations about politics and history. I appreciate your mentorship and always enjoyed our talks in your office. I learned so much about English and grammar while working with you. You are an amazing educator and have inspired generations of students to embody core values of integrity, respect, personal growth, community, and wisdom. I am forever grateful.

I appreciate Mr. Bausch and Mr. Dominguez for having taught and fostered my love of speech and debate. We have analyzed text, studied public speaking styles, debated current events, and explored the best way to present complex arguments. You helped me understand the contributions of gifted orators to history and the knowledge I learned in your class was the inspiration to write this book. Thank you to Ms. Scobie for all of your guidance, support, and encouragement. I hope we are in touch for a long time to come.

I am thankful for having had the opportunity to learn from everyone who let me intern for them. You taught me volumes about professionalism, politics, business, economics, finance, public policy, how to respect differing views, lifelong learning, and a strong work ethic.

Thank you to Skyhorse for taking a chance on a young author. I appreciate how your company is committed to expressing views from both sides of the political spectrum. Healthy debate with a bipartisan spirit is fundamental to American democracy. I am grateful to everyone who helped me edit the book, offered suggestions, and made the manuscript better.

I'd also like to acknowledge you—the reader—for taking the time to read this book. I hope you found the lessons valuable. Whenever politics or the national mood gets too heated, I hope you refer back to *The Missing Center* as a reminder of how to restore civility in public discourse and how, by working together, America has solved challenges of the past and has the ability to do so in the future as well. My generation has grown up in a time of increased partisanship and a challenging political climate. This book reminds us that we have the tools to forge a better path forward.

BIBLIOGRAPHY

9/11 Memorial & Museum. "Commemoration." 9/11 Memorial & Museum. Accessed March 5, 2024. https://www.911memorial.org/connect/commemoration.

Adams, Michael. "Federal Funds Rate History 1990 to 2023." Forbes. March 21, 2024. https://www.forbes.com/advisor/investing/fed-funds-rate-history/.

American Psychological Association. "Misinformation and Disinformation." American Psychology Association Psychology Topics: Journalism and Facts. 2024. https://www.apa.org/topics/journalism-facts/misinformation-disinformation.

Anonymous Whistleblower and Whistleblower Aid. "Re: Supplemental Disclosure of Securities Law Violations by Facebook, Inc. (NASDAQ: FB), SEC TCR #[Redacted]." The Facebook Papers (2021): 10. Accessed at https://facebookpapers.com/sec-documents/.

Aon. "Aon: U.S. Employer Health Care Costs Projected to Increase 8.5 Percent Next Year." August 22, 2023. https://aon.mediaroom.com/2023-08-22-Aon-U-S-Employer-Health-Care-Costs-Projected-to-Increase-8-5-Percent-Next-Year.

Barrett, Paul M. "Fueling the Fire: How Social Media Intensifies U.S. Political Polarization—And What Can Be Done About It." NYU Stern Center for Business and Human Rights. September 2021. https://bhr.stern.nyu.edu/publication/fueling-the-fire-how-social-media-intensifies-u-s-political-polarization-and-what-can-be-done-about-it/.

Barrett, Paul, Justin Hendrix, and Grant Sims. "How Tech Platforms Fuel U.S. Political Polarization and What Government Can Do About It." The Brookings Institution. September 27, 2021. https://www.brookings.edu/articles/how-tech-platforms-fuel-u-s-political-polarization-and-what-government-can-do-about-it/.

Biden, Joseph. "Inaugural Address by President Joseph R. Biden, Jr." Speech, Washington, D.C., January 21, 2021. The White House. https://www.whitehouse.gov/briefing-room/speeches-remarks/2021/01/20/inaugural-address-by-president-joseph-r-biden-jr/.

Biden, Joseph. "Remarks by President Biden to Mark One Year Since the January 6th Deadly Assault on the U.S. Capitol." Speech, Washington, D.C., January 6, 2022. The White House. https://www.whitehouse.gov/briefing-room/speeches-remarks/2022/01/06/remarks-by-president-biden-to-mark-one-year-since-the-january-6th-deadly-assault-on-the-u-s-capitol/

Blackford, Sheila. "Disputed Election of 1876." Miller Center. Accessed May 16, 2024. https://millercenter.org/the-presidency/educational-resources/disputed-election-1876.

Bush, George W. "2002 State of the Union Address." Speech, Washington, D.C., January 29, 2002. U.S. National Archives and Records Administration. https://georgewbush-whitehouse.archives.gov/news/releases/2002/01/20020129-11.html.

Bush, George W. "President Bush Calls for New Palestinian Leadership." Speech, Washington, D.C., June 24, 2002. U.S. National Archives and Records Administration. https://georgewbush-whitehouse.archives.gov/news/releases/2002/06/20020624-3.html.

Bush, George W. "President Highlights Progress in Education Reform." Speech, Washington, D.C., June 10, 2003. U.S. National Archives and Records Administration. https://georgewbush-whitehouse.archives.gov/news/releases/2003/06/20030610-4.html.

Bush, George W. "President's Radio Address," November 22, 2003. U.S. National Archives and Records Administration. Transcript. https://georgewbush-whitehouse.archives.gov/news/releases/2003/11/20031122-6.html.

Civiqs. "Report: Americans Support Universal Pre-K and Free Community College," May 12, 2021, https://civiqs.com/reports/2021/5/12/report-americans-support-universal-pre-k-and-free-community-college.

Claxton, Gary, and Matthew Rae. "What Are the Recent Trends in Employer-Based Health Coverage?" Peterson KFF Health System Tracker. December 22, 2023. https://www. healthsystemtracker.org/chart-collection/trends-in-employer-based-health-coverage/.

Clinton, Hillary. "Remarks at the UN Commission on the Status of Women." Speech, New York City, New York, March 12, 2010. U.S. Department of State. https://2009-2017.state.gov/secretary/20092013clinton/rm/2010/03/138320.htm.

Clinton, Hillary. "Remarks in Recognition of International Human Rights Day." Speech, Geneva, Switzerland, December 6, 2011. U.S. Department of State. https://2009-2017.state.gov/secretary/20092013clinton/rm/2011/12/178368.htm

Clinton, William J. "Remarks by the President at America's Millennium Gala." Speech, Washington, D.C., December 31, 1999. U.S. National Archives and Records Administration. https://clintonwhitehouse4. Archives.gov/WH/New/html/20000104.html.

Cohen, Sandy. "The fastest vaccine in history." UCLA Health. December 10, 2020. https://www.uclahealth.org/news/article/the-fastest-vaccine-in-history.

Congress.gov, Raphael Warnock. "Info—S.283—118th Congress (2023-2024): Headway Act." Congress.gov. www.congress.gov/bill/118th-congress/senate-bill/2832/all-info.

Cummings, Jeanne. "2008 Campaign Costliest in U.S. History." Politico. November 5, 2008. https://www.politico.com/story/2008/11/2008-campaign-costliest-in-us-history-015283.

Desilver, Drew. "Trump's Victory Another Example of How Electoral College Wins Are Bigger than Popular Vote Ones." Pew Research Center. December 20, 2016. https://www.pewresearch.org/short-reads/2016/12/20/why-electoral-college-landslides-are-easier-to-win-than-popular-vote-ones/.

Dizikes, Peter. "Study: On Twitter, False News Travels Faster than True Stories." MIT News. March 8, 2018. https://news. mit.edu/2018/study-twitter-false-news-travels-faster-true-stories-0308.

Economic Cooperation Foundation. "Second Intifada (Al Aqsa Intifada, 2000–2005?)." The Israeli-Palestinian Conflict: An Interactive Database. Accessed May 16, 2024. https://ecf.org.il/issues/issue/230.

Finkel, Eli J., et al., "Political Sectarianism in America," *Science* 370, no. 6516 (October 2020): 533-536.

Flake, Jeff. 115th Cong., 1st sess., *Congressional Record* 163 (daily ed. October 24, 2017): S6735:S6736.

Gallup. "Abortion." Gallup Historical Trends. May 1, 2023. https://news.gallup.com/poll/1576/abortion.aspx

Gallup. "Healthcare System." Gallup Historical Trends. 2024. https://news.gallup.com/poll/4708/healthcare-system.aspx.

Gallup. "LGBTQ+ Rights." Gallup Historical Trends. May 28, 2023. https://news.gallup.com/poll/1651/gay-lesbian-rights.aspx.

Gallup. "Medicare." Gallup Historical Trends. 2024. https://news.gallup.com/poll/14596/medicare.aspx.

Gao, George, and Samantha Smith. "Presidential Job Approval Ratings from Ike to Obama." Pew Research Center. January 12, 2016. https://www.pewresearch.org/short-reads/2016/01/12/presidential-job-approval-ratings-from-ike-to-obama/.

Henry J. Kaiser Family Foundation and Harvard School of Public Health. "New Survey Finds Majority of Seniors Want Congress to Pass a Medicare Drug Bill This Year, but Most Worry They Will Still Pay Too Much Even If Congress Acts." September 3, 2003. https://www.kff.org/wp-content/uploads/2013/01/new-survey-finds-majority-of-seniors-want-congress-to-pass-a-medicare-drug-bill-this-year-but-most-worry-they-will-still-pay-too-much-even-if-congress.pdf.

Hernandez, Erik L., and Kevin McElrath. "Public and Private Preschool Enrollment from 2019 to 2021 at its Lowest Since 2005." U.S. Census Bureau. August 30, 2023. https://www.census.gov/library/stories/2023/08/preschool-enrollment.html.

Hess, Frederick M. "Accountability Without Angst? Public Opinion and No Child Left Behind." American Enterprise Institute. December 29, 2006. https://www.aei.org/articles/accountability-without-angst-public-opinion-and-no-child-left-behind/

Hillman, Nick. "Party Control in Congress and State Legislatures (1978-2016)." University of Wisconsin–Madison. February 1, 2017. https://web.education.wisc.edu/nwhillman/index.php/2017/02/01/party-control-in-congress-and-state-legislatures/.

Just Security. "Disinformation, Radicalization, and Algorithmic Amplification: What Steps Can Congress Take?." February 7, 2022. https://www.justsecurity.org/79995/disinformation-radicalization-and-algorithmic-amplification-what-steps-can-congress-take/.

Karoly, Lynn A., and Jill S. Cannon. "Making Preschool Investments Count Through the American Families Plan." June 3, 2021. https://www.rand.org/pubs/commentary/2021/06/making-preschool-investments-count-through-the-american.html.

KFF. "KFF Health Tracking Poll: The Public's Views on the ACA." May 15, 2024. https://www.kff.org/interactive/kff-health-tracking-poll-the-publics-views-on-the-aca/#?response=Favorable--Unfavorable&aRange=all.

Kleinfeld, Rachel. "Polarization, Democracy, and Political Violence in the United States: What the Research Says." Carnegie Endowment for International Peace. September 5, 2023. https://carnegieendowment.org/research/2023/09/polarization-democracy-and-political-violence-in-the-united-states-what-the-research-says?lang=en.

Mann, Thomas E. "Reflections on the 2000 U.S. Presidential Election." Brookings Institute. January 1, 2001, https://www.brookings.edu/articles/reflections-on-the-2000-u-s-presidential-election/.

Medicare Prescription Drug and Modernization Act of 2003, HR.1, 108th Cong., 2nd Sess., *Congressional Record* 149, pt. 13: 17213–14.

Obama, Barack. "Osama Bin Laden Dead." Speech, Washington, D.C., May 2, 2011. U.S. National Archives and Records Administration. https://obamawhitehouse.archives.gov/blog/2011/05/02/osama-bin-laden-dead.

Obama, Barack. "President Barack Obama's Inaugural Address." Speech, Washington, D.C., January 21, 2009. U.S. National Archives and Records Administration. https://obamawhitehouse.archives.gov/blog/2009/01/21/president-Barack-obamas-inaugural-address

Obama, Barack. "Remarks by the President on the Affordable Care Act." Speech, Miami, Florida, October 20, 2016. U.S. National Archives and Records Administration. https://obamawhitehouse.archives.gov/the-press-office/2016/10/20/remarks-president-affordable-care-act.

Obama, Barack. "Remarks by the President on the Mortgage Crisis." Speech, Mesa, Arizona, February 18, 2009. U.S. National Archives and Records Administration. https://obamawhitehouse.archives.gov/the-press-office/remarks-president-mortgage-crisis.

Obama, Barack. "United States Health Care Reform Progress to Date and Next Steps." *Journal of the American Medical Association (JAMA)* 316 no. 5 (July 2016): 525–32.

Pelosi, Nancy. "Transcript of Speaker Pelosi's Remarks at Weekly Press Conference." Speech, Washington, D.C., June 24, 2022. Congresswoman Nancy Pelosi. https://pelosi.house. gov/news/ press-releases/transcript-of-speaker-pelosi-s-remarks-at-weekly-press-conference-14.

Pew Research Center, "Support for Same-Sex Marriage Grows, Even Among Groups That Had Been Skeptical," June 26, 2017, https:// www.pewresearch.org/politics/2017/06/26/support-for-same-sex-marriage-grows-even-among-groups-that-had-been-skeptical/

Powell, Jerome. "Transcript of Chair Powell's Press Conference, May 3, 2023." Speech, Washington, D.C., May 3, 2023. Board of Governors of the Federal Reserve System. https://www.federalreserve.gov/mediacenter/files/FOMCpresconf20230503.pdf.

Rogers, John, Bo Sun, and Chris Webster. "US-China Tensions." VoxChina. April 28, 2021. https://www.voxchina.org/show-3-227.html.

Sinema, Kyrsten "Sinema Statement on Jeff Flake's Unanimous Confirmation as U.S. Ambassador to Turkey," October 27, 2021, https://www.sinema.senate.gov/sinema-statement-jeff-flakes-unanimous-confirmation-us-ambassador-turkey/.

Stanford, Libby. "Which States Offer Universal Pre-K? It's More Complicated Than You Might Think." EducationWeek. January 25, 2023. https://www.edweek.org/teaching-learning/which-states-offer-universal-pre-k-its-more-complicated-than-you-might-think/2023/01.

Trump, Donald. "2017 Inaugural Address." Speech, Washington, D.C., January 20, 2017. U.S. National Archives and Records Administration. https://trumpwhitehouse.archives.gov/briefings-statements/the-inaugural-address/

Trump, Donald. "Remarks by President Trump at the Operation Warp Speed Vaccine Summit." Speech, Washington, D.C., December 8, 2020. U.S. National Archives and Records Administration. https://trumpwhitehouse.archives.gov/briefings-statements/remarks-president-trump-operation-warp-speed-vaccine-summit/.

United Nations Security Council. "General Assembly Resolution 181 (II). Future Government of Palestine." The United Nations. November 29, 1947. https://www.un.org/unispal/document/auto-insert-185393/

United States Attorney's Office. "30 Months Since the Jan. 6 Attack on the Capitol." U.S. Department of Justice. July 6, 2023. https://www.justice.gov/usao-dc/30-months-jan-6-attack-capitol.

United States Bureau of Labor Statistics. "12-Month Percentage Change, Consumer Price Index, Selected Categories, Not Seasonally Adjusted" all items, last updated April 2024, https://www.bls.gov/charts/consumer-price-index/consumer-price-index-by-category-line-chart.htm.

United States Bureau of Labor Statistics. "Spotlight on Statistics: The Recession of 2007-2009." February 2012. https://www.bls.gov/spotlight/2012/recession/pdf/recession_bls_spotlight.pdf.

United States Department of Education Press Office. "Biden-Harris Administration Releases Resources to Support Preschool Expansion and Early School Success." U.S. Department of Education. February 26, 2024. https://www.ed.gov/news/press-releases/biden-harris-administration-releases-resources-support-pre-school-expansion-and-early-school-success.

United States Department of State, Office of the Historian, Foreign Service Institute. "The Oslo Accords and the Arab-Israeli Peace Process." 2000. https://history.state.gov/milestones/1993-2000/oslo.

United States Department of the Treasury. "Troubled Asset Relief Program (TARP)." 2023. https://home.treasury.gov/data/troubled-asset-relief-program.

University of Missouri–Columbia. "Presidential Candidates' Television Ads Most Negative In History." ScienceDaily. November 1, 2008. www.sciencedaily.com/releases/2008/10/081031102057.htm.

University of Wisconsin–Madison and Texas A & M University. "Top 100 Speeches of the Twentieth Century." University of Wisconsin–Madison. 1999. https://news.wisc.edu/i-have-a-dream-leads-top-100-speeches-of-the-century/.

Warnock, Raphael. "Video: Head Start Alumnus Senator Reverend Warnock Keynotes at National Head Start Association Conference, Introduces Legislation to Increase Access to Early Head Start Programs." Speech, Washington, D.C., September 18, 2023. Reverend Raphael Warnock, U.S. Senator for Georgia. https://www.warnock.senate.gov/newsroom/press-releases/video-head-start-alumnus-senator-reverend-warnock-keynotes-at-national-head-start-association-conference-introduces-legislation-to-increase-access-to-early-head-start-p/.

Warren, Elizabeth. "Senator Warren's Remarks at the Edward M. Kennedy Institute for the United States Senate." Speech, Washington, D.C., September 27, 2015. Elizabeth Warren Newsroom. https://www.warren.senate.gov/newsroom/press-releases/senator-warren-and-039s-remarks-at-the-edward-m-kennedy-institute-for-the-united-states-senate.

Weinberg, John. "The Great Recession and Its Aftermath." Federal Reserve History. November 22, 2013. https://www. federalreservehistory.org/essays/great-recession-and-its-aftermath.

West, Darrell M. "A Report on the 2008 Presidential Nomination Ads: Ads More Negative than Previous Years." The Brookings Institution. July 2, 2008. https://www.brookings.edu/articles/a-report-on-the-2008-presidential-nomination-ads-ads-more-negative-than-previous-years/.

White House Office of the Press Secretary. "Fact Sheet: Seven Years Ago, the American Reinvestment and Recovery Act Helped Bring Our Economy Back from the Brink of a Second Great Depression." The White House Briefing Room. February 25, 2016. https://obamawhitehouse. archives.gov/the-press-office/2016/02/25/fact-sheet-seven-years-ago-american-recovery-and-reinvestment-act-helped.

Yeban, Jade. "Criticism of No Child Left Behind." FindLaw. November 8, 2023. https://www.findlaw.com/education/curriculum-standards-school-funding/criticism-of-no-child-left-behind.html.

Yellen, Janet L. "Remarks by Secretary of the Treasury Janet L. Yellen on the U.S.-China Economic Relationship at Johns Hopkins School of Advanced International Studies." Speech, Washington, D.C., April 20, 2023. U.S. Department of the Treasury. https://home.treasury.gov/news/press-releases/jy14

Zou, Jie Jenny, and Erin B. Logan. "Jan. 6: By the Numbers." The Chronicle. January 5, 2022. https://chronline.com/stories/jan-6-by-the-numbers,282020.

NOTES

NOTES

NOTES

NOTES

NOTES

NOTES

NOTES

NOTES

NOTES

NOTES

NOTES